Q   SY
R

QUICK AND EASY HOME REPAIR

WRITTEN & ILLUSTRATED BY

Graham Blackburn

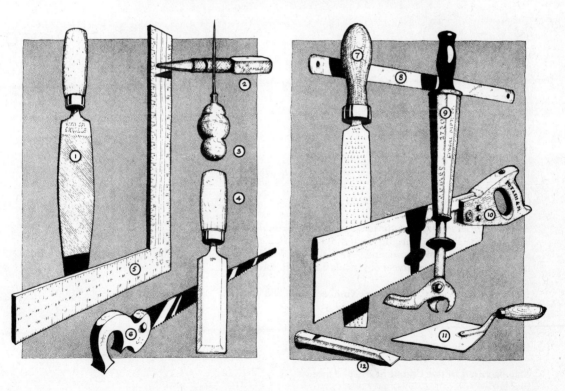

Ballantine Books · New York

Library of Congress Catalog Card Number: 85-90883

ISBN: 0-345-33035-8

Cover design by James R. Harris

Manufactured in the United States of America

First Edition: June 1986

10 9 8 7 6 5 4 3 2 1

For my friends

Basia and Peter Kaminski,
Paul Cohen, George James, and David Ryon,
John and Hilda Cranfield,
my parents John and Verena Blackburn,
and also William Oberheim
and Christopher David

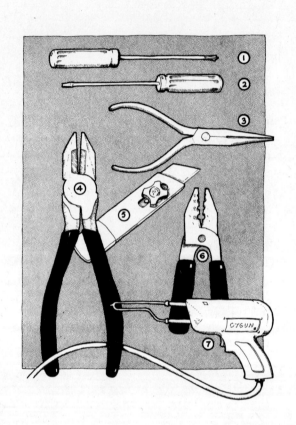

CONTENTS

PREFACE

This is a book of first aid for your home, its inside and its outside. *Quick and Easy Home Repair* is designed to show you what you can do when you come home and find yourself faced with a problem that must be dealt with at once. There are at the same time many other problems that develop gradually, often over months or even years. You should be able to see these coming and prevent them with a program of preventive maintenance, such as that described in my earlier book, *A Calendar of Home Repair*. However, no matter how well you prepare, there will always be the unexpected disaster about which *something* must be done at once. This book will show you how.

The subjects covered are not, of course, *everything* that can go wrong with a house or an apartment, but they are the most common problems which demand immediate attention. Many repairs are best left to professionals, and require a more thorough remedy than is described here, but *Quick and Easy Home Repair* will get you through the worst of it—and prevent the situation from deteriorating.

Not much skill is needed, just willingness and a few basic tools that every house should have, such as screwdrivers, a hammer, a putty knife, and the odd tool that can be readily found at the corner hardware store when the need arises.

The book is divided into four parts in order to make it easier to find the solution to your problem: Part One contains structural problems with the woodwork, walls, floors, windows and doors, etc.; Part Two deals with electrical problems; Part Three covers common plumbing emergencies; and Part Four is concerned with the heating and cooling systems of your home.

Within each part you will also find "fact" pages that provide not solutions to specific problems but helpful general information, relative to that part—such as the various types of wire available, the different types of electrical outlets you might need, extra tools, etc.

At the end of the book you will find an index, and a place to write the names and telephone numbers of the people you'll need in situations that require more help than you are able to render yourself. But always, before calling for outside help, look the situation over yourself instead of immediately declaring, "The water's out—call the plumber!" You will be surprised at what you can fix yourself, often faster and cheaper, with a little patience and some understanding of the problem. This book should help.

Graham Blackburn
The Crown & Anchor
Woodstock, New York

PART ONE

STRUCTURAL REPAIRS

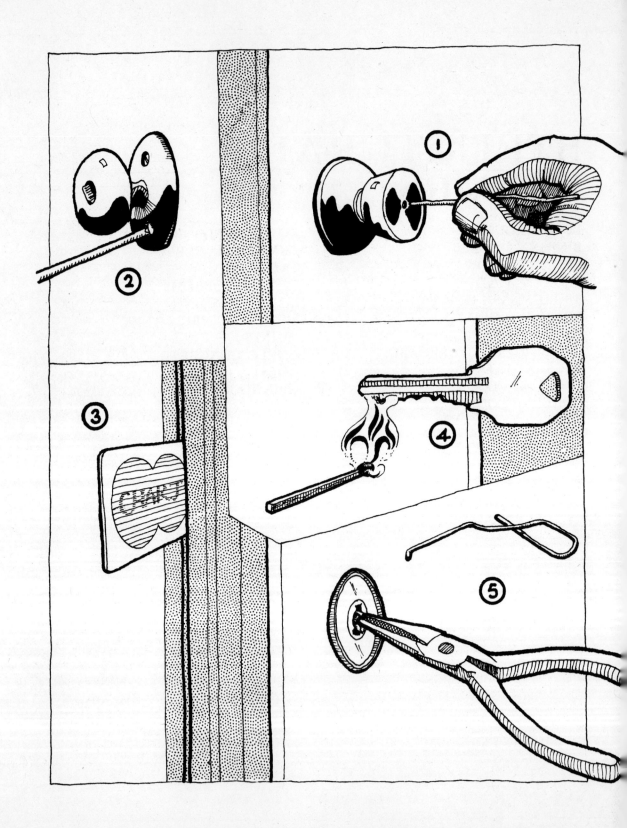

LOCKED OUT!

If the bathroom door or the bedroom door locks when it shouldn't and you have to open it from the outside, there are several things you can do. Many modern bathroom door locks have a slot or hole in the outside knob. If you stick a thin piece of wire ① into the hole and simply push hard, or stick a small screwdriver into the slot, and simply turn it, you can usually release the lock. If you're stuck on the inside you can disassemble the whole doorknob, since the screws that hold it together are on this side ②. Pull out the knob and you will be able to poke around inside and turn the bolt.

A word of warning: never oil your locks—the oil only collects dust and eventually gums up the works! Lubricate by all means, but use a little graphite or a silicone type spray—never household oil.

Sometimes it is possible to slide something thin but fairly rigid, like a credit card ③, between the door and the doorstop, pushing back the striker bolt and thereby opening the door. A door equipped with a deadbolt lock, of course, is designed to prevent this, forcing you to try some other solution—such as removing the hinges. If you can see the back of the hinge, the chances are that you can remove the hinge pin (see page 7) by tapping it out with a hammer and screwdriver. Now you can open the door from the hinge side!

If you live where it gets cold you may encounter the frozen lock, or even the lock that has been iced over by freezing rain. Here you must chip away all the ice and try to get the key in and turn without breaking it. If it commonly gets cold where you live you may well have one of the little spray de-icers used for car doors in your car, but if you don't, most of the other remedies will not be much use

since you won't be able to get into the house to avail yourself of them. It's often easier to find a match or cigarette lighter. Try heating the key ④ and working it in slowly, bit by bit. You may have to do this quite a few times, but eventually the heat from the key will thaw out the lock enough to let it turn. Once in, make sure you spray the lock with some silicone, which not only lubricates but also keeps moisture out—it's the frozen moisture that causes the trouble.

Then there is the problem of the key breaking off in the lock! If you can get to the other side of the door you can remove the cylinder and easily push the broken key out. But if you're stuck on the outside you must try to remove the key, either with a pair of needle-nose pliers or a thin piece of wire, such as a paper clip, bent over at the end to form a small hook ⑤. There is often room above the irregular edge of the key to hook the wire into and then gently pull.

If the key was fully inserted before it broke, you may still be able to open the lock simply by inserting a screwdriver into the key slot, and turning.

If you absolutely can't get the key out, try one of the procedures for opening a locked door (covered above). Failing all else you can always break a window and let yourself in—and then repair the glass (as described later in the book).

If you should lose a key, remember that it is always possible to have a locksmith make a new one, and if circumstances permit, even come in person and open the lock for you. This is rarely convenient, however, and always expensive. A better idea is to leave a spare key with a trusted neighbor.

5

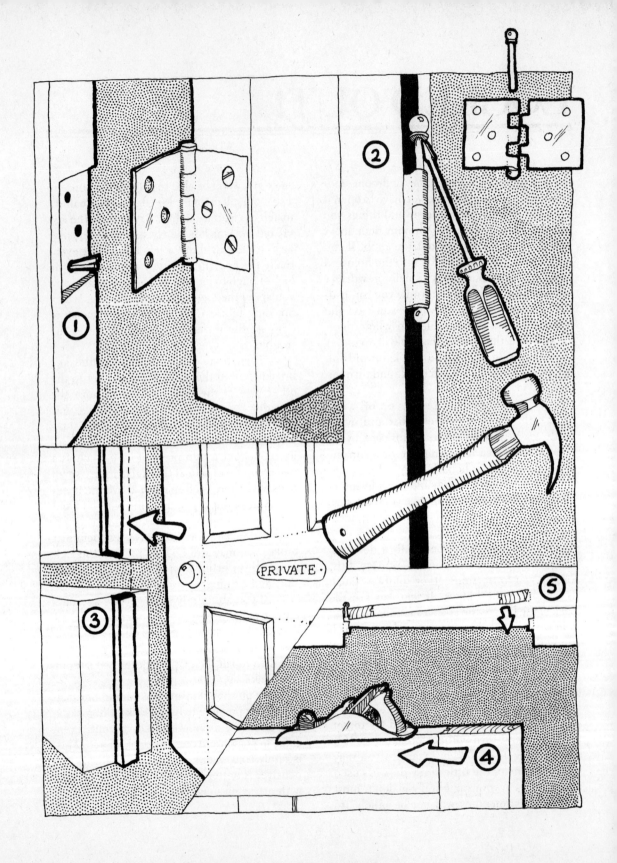

PRIVATE

BINDING DOOR

Doors often become infuriatingly difficult to open—or close—and although the repair of a door can require a fair amount of carpentry skill, there are a few very simple things you can try before calling in expensive help.

One of the more common reasons that doors stick is that the hinges work loose. The actual hinge-leaves and the pin that holds them may wear so much that they need to be replaced, but more commonly the screws holding the hinges simply work loose and must be retightened. Before you do anything else, get out the screwdriver and make sure that all the screws are in flush with the hinge—and tight. If they have been loose for a while the chances are that they will have made the screw holes too big to keep them tight. One cure is to remove the hinge and plug up the screw holes with matchsticks ①. Or, whittle a piece of wood to fit, and dip it in glue before pushing it in. Trim off any wood sticking out with a chisel and replace the hinge.

If the hinge is stiff to operate, try to get it to work easily. Remove the pin ② and rub off any rust or accumulated paint. Then smear a little petroleum jelly on the pin before replacing it. If it has become bent you should try to straighten it, because a bent pin can also make the door hard to open.

Frequent repainting can increase the size of a door enough to cause it to stick in its frame. If this is the case, get out the sandpaper and rub down the edges of the door and the inside of the frame. If you get down to bare wood there should be enough space left to put back on one coat of paint to match the rest of the door. Doors in older apartment buildings are notorious victims of paint buildup, and often the best plan is to strip the whole door.

Too much paint or simply excessive moisture can reduce the clearance between the door and the doorstop. (The doorstop is the narrow strip fastened to the inside of the door frame against which the door actually stops.) Rather than resorting to radical surgery on the door, or even a complete paint-stripping job, it may be simpler to pry off the doorstop and nail it back on, but set a little further away from the door ③. If you have a painted door, however, this will probably chip the paint enough to make you want to paint the door again anyway.

You shouldn't overlook the possibility that some part of the door's weatherstripping has become misplaced, and is now causing opening and closing problems.

If the door has warped or swollen, or if the building has shifted enough to distort the frame, the only cure may be to refit the door. The tools to use are a rasp or file, and a plane. But before you start removing too much wood from the door, remember the following points: plane *in* from the ends to avoid splitting off the corners ④; plane the hinge side rather than the lock side because it is a lot easier to reset hinges than to refit locks; the lock side (if you must plane here) is bevelled towards the edge that closes ⑤ (as is the bottom of the door sometimes). Check *frequently* to see if you have removed enough wood; it is hard to glue pieces back on.

STUCK WINDOW

Of the two most common types of windows, double-hung sash windows and casement windows, the former is more prone to sticking. Since windows are exposed to the weather they are frequently painted, and the resulting paint buildup can effectively seal a window shut. While this may be good insulation and draft prevention it's not much good if you want to open the window.

Sometimes just running a razor knife around the paint "seal" between the window and the stop will free it up, but more often than not you will have to take a broad knife, such as a putty knife (never use a screwdriver, which will mar the wood or metal), and work it in gently the whole way around the window ①, both inside and outside. If this doesn't work, try prying up the window with something broad and strong, like an axe head ②. Work evenly; it's no good just prying up one side, for this will tilt the window in its frame and wedge it even tighter. Work both sides evenly. If the window is already open, but stuck, try closing it from above. Don't pull down on the bottom part or push up on the top part—if the window is stuck hard enough you may break the frame.

If the above procedure fails, you'll have to try something a little more complicated: removing the window stops and possibly the parting strip. Pry off the stop molding carefully, using a chisel inserted as close as possible to the small nails that hold the stop on ③. This will minimize any tendency for the stop to split. If just the lower sash is stuck you will now be able to remove it and clean or sand the edges so that it slides easily up and down when replaced. If the upper sash is stuck then you must remove the *parting strip* as well. This is the narrow piece that separates the two sashes, and usually is not nailed in. You can pull it straight out using a pair of pliers—but use a small block of wood on either side (as shown—④) in order not to damage it.

If removing the dirt and excess paint does not allow the window to slide freely, replace the parting strip and the stop. Then force a block of wood, slightly wider than the gap between them into the groove, and hammer it up and down. For even more space, replace the stop further out than its original position.

Along with this cleaning, lubricating with a silicone stick lubricant often helps. This is good for wood as well as metal windows. Windows that slide on aluminum can be made to work more smoothly by rubbing the aluminum with fine wire wool.

Casement windows that stick may be dealt with in the same way as binding doors (see the previous section), although sometimes the reason you can't get a casement window open is that the hardware that opens and closes it is stiff. If you have a rod-and-pivot assembly, make sure the screws are tight, clean the rod with fine wire wool, and lubricate it lightly with paraffin. A cranking assembly usually balks because it is dirty. Clean it out with a vacuum cleaner and a piece of thin wire so that the channels are all unclogged. Then lubricate it at least once a year.

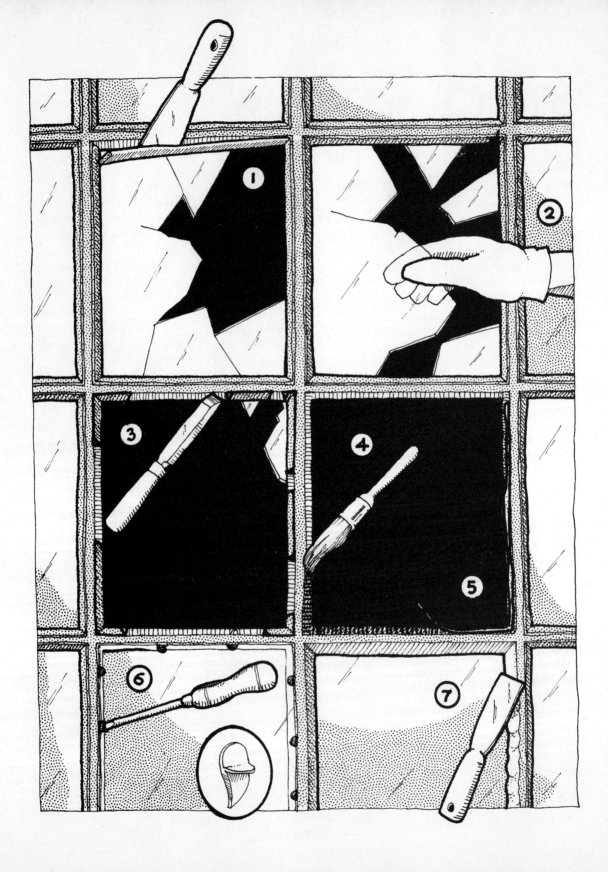

BROKEN WINDOW

The first step is to remove the broken glass. If the glass is held in place by wooden strips all you have to do is to pry these off ①. If they are painted you will make a neater job by first scoring the paint seal with a razor knife. Pry the strips off with a putty knife ①. Note that one of them fits with a butt joint against the others, which are all mitered, so pry the butt-jointed one off first.

If the glass is held in place with putty or glazing compound, wear gloves and pull the glass out piece by piece ②. If the glass is merely cracked, you must make a hole. You will make less of a mess if before hitting the glass with a hammer you stick some masking tape on the glass and hit it there.

When all the glass has been removed, clean out the rebate (channel) in which the glass sat. If putty was used it may have become very hard. You'll need to use something strong, like an old chisel ③ to get all the pieces out. Make sure that you remove any glazing points or brads that may have been used to hold the glass in place, and try not to gouge the wood.

The next stage is frequently forgotten but is very worthwhile: prime the now bare wood of the rebate with paint or linseed oil ④. This protects the wood from moisture and will help prevent deterioration of the new glazing.

Unless the broken piece of glass is extremely large, such as in a sliding glass door (in which case you should leave its repair to a professional), you will be able to replace it with a new piece cut to size at the local hardware store. Measure the opening very carefully and get a piece of glass that is ⅛ inch smaller in both length and breadth.

Before inserting the new glass, press a bead of putty or other glazing compound into the corner of the rebate ⑤. This will act both as a seal and as a cushion against any irregularities in the frame, so it does not need to be a very thick bead.

Now insert the glass and, while holding it firmly against the bead of compound, push in glazing points ⑥ every 6 inches or so to hold the glass tightly against its frame. Although the glazing points must be inserted snugly against the glass, be careful not to push too hard or you might crack the new glass. Make sure that they go in deeply enough to be covered by the compound that will hold the glass in place.

This step is omitted, of course, if the glass is held in place not by putty but by the wooden strips shown in ①. Instead, simply replace the wooden strips in their original position, and in reverse order.

Whether you use real putty or a glazing compound make sure that it's really soft before you start—and keep the lid on the can so the contents do not dry out. Roll some between your hands into a long thin sausage and press this firmly into place with the flat of the putty knife. Then, pressing firmly and keeping the knife at a constant angle, draw the knife across the compound, trimming off any excess and leaving a smooth surface behind ⑦. It helps to keep one corner of the knife just touching the glass and the other corner over the edge of the window frame. Be patient at the corners.

Finally, having allowed the compound to dry until it is no longer soft and sticky to the touch (this can take up to a week, depending on the weather), paint it the same color as the window, carefully overlapping the glass by about 1/16 inch to make a weather seal. Resist the temptation to clean any putty smudges off the glass until the paint is dry, or you will spoil the looks and effectiveness of the job.

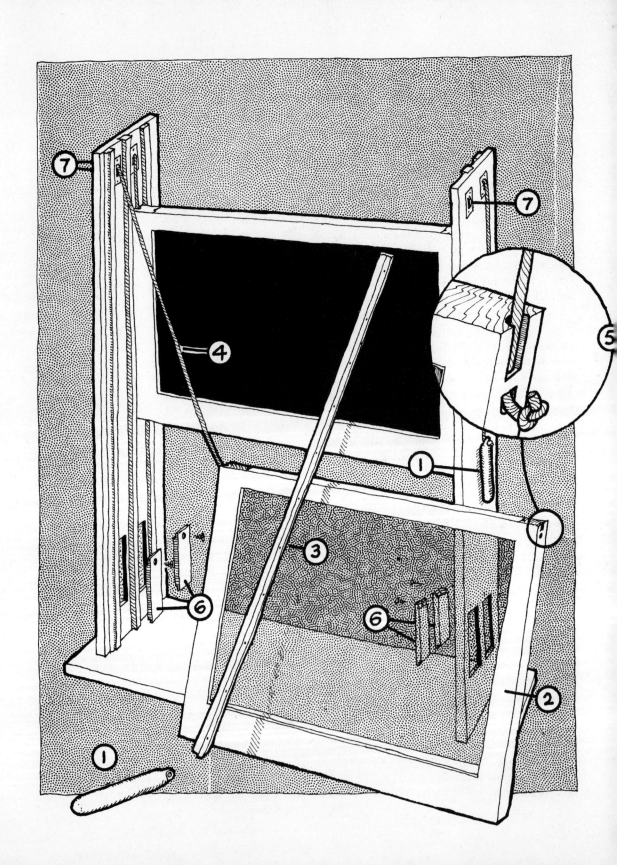

BROKEN SASH CORD

Modern double-hung windows slide up and down on aluminum tracks, the sideways pressure of which is enough to support the window in any position. Older windows use heavy sash weights ① to counterbalance them in any required position. When one of the cords that attaches the weights to the actual window (properly called the sash ②) breaks, the window will no longer stay up and the cords must be replaced.

The first step is to carefully remove the window stop ③ on the side with the broken cord. The stop is held in place by small nails. Pry this stop up by inserting a broad blade under it, as near to the nails as possible. You can now pull the lower sash from its frame—although it will still be attached to the unbroken cord and weight ④. If, indeed, it is the upper sash which has a broken cord, you will still have to remove the lower sash first. In this case it might be easier to store the lower sash out of the way. The cord is usually attached by being threaded through a pocket in the side of the sash and having a knot tied in its end to prevent it from pulling through ⑤.

To remove the upper sash, pull out the parting strip with pliers. Put scraps of wood on either side of the parting strip to avoid chewing up the wood with the jaws of the pliers (see ④, page 9). Because these parting strips are very occasionally nailed or screwed in place, check for nails or screws carefully before you start pulling. Now the upper sash can be freed.

The next step is to recover the weight. This will usually have fallen down to the bottom of the box, inside the window frame, and can be retrieved through an access panel ⑥ near the bottom of the window. These panels are usually held in place with a screw which is often obscured by several layers of paint, as indeed may be the whole outline of the access panel. Scratch around until you find the panel and remove it. Be prepared to finish sawing the panel out with a thin keyhole saw—many windows are built with the access panel only partly cut out.

Pull out the weight and untie the remains of the broken sash cord. Next, thread a new length of cord through the pulley ⑦ at the top of the window and feed it down inside the window until you can pull it out of the access panel and tie it onto the weight. This threading business can be facilitated by first hanging some washers on the end of the new sash cord, and securing the other end so it doesn't slip through the pulley hole!

Use the old length of cord to determine the length of the new piece, and then make it about 2 inches shorter to allow for stretching. Now attach the free end of the cord to the sash and slide the sash up and down in its tracks. If it's the upper sash, check that when it is raised fully, the weight hangs at least 3 inches above the sill (you can check this by looking through the access panel). If it's the lower sash, check that it can be lowered all the way in its frame—if not, the sash cord is too short.

If everything works fine, take this opportunity to check the condition of the other sash cords. Chain can also be used to replace the cords, though it is rather noisy and can get rusty on you. But in any event replace anything that looks worn.

Finally, put everything back together in the reverse order from which it is disassembled, taking special care not to nail the window stop on too close to (or the window won't slide) or too far from (or the window will rattle) the replaced sash.

LEAKY WINDOW

A poorly constructed window can leak air in (and heat out) and can also allow rain and snow in. This is not only uncomfortable but can also be damaging—both to the window and to the surrounding walls.

If during or after a heavy rainstorm you notice wetness around the window, especially in the adjacent walls, water is probably getting in between the window frame and the siding. The immediate cure is to caulk around the frame, making sure that the caulk penetrates any gaps that may exist between the frame and the siding ①.

A more lasting solution is to remove the outside trim and make sure that there is a layer of building paper extending from under the immediate siding up to the actual window frame. If necessary, gently pry up the ends of the siding and insert a strip of building paper underneath ②. Window trim either covers the ends of the siding, or is nailed directly to the house's sheathing (the inside skin of the house) with the siding butting up against it. The latter method, if done carefully, can provide the best seal, but builders often find it quicker just to run the siding up somewhere near the window opening and cover the consequent irregular edge with the window trim. The trim-over method requires more thorough caulking.

While this applies to wood houses, brick and stone houses, whether they have wooden or metal window frames, must also be carefully caulked at the joints (as in ①). Water can enter here and seep along inside to appear somewhere else in the wall. While it is possible that the actual walls are leaking, you should check the window frame first.

Another area of the window that is susceptible to leaking is along the top of the outside frame. This should be fitted with a drip cap ③ and be properly flashed. If the drip cap has shrunk away from the siding or broken off in part or whole the gap can be caulked as a temporary measure, but the cap should be properly replaced. In wood houses replacement involves the removal of the siding immediately above the window ④, because the drip cap's upper edge must fit *under* the siding. Just as at the sides of the window, building paper ⑤ should extend under the window trim. A metal flashing ⑥ of aluminum, or better still, copper (since it lasts longer), must be fitted *under* the siding and *over* the drip cap. If the flashing is nailed in place with nails of a dissimilar metal, galvanic action will eventually result in a leak at these spots.

Improperly sloped or damaged window sills can also trap water or snow and lead it into the house. The replacement of the window sill involves some serious carpentry, but caulking can still offer a temporary solution.

If you have wooden double-hung sash windows, check that the exterior window stops are nailed tightly to the frame, especially if the window is unpainted.

Finally, check the glazing compound around the glass ⑦. If this is cracked or partly missing, water can enter here and will stain (and eventually rot) the inside of the window. This is especially prevalent with unpainted wooden windows, since there is no paint to act as an extra seal over the glazing and the glass.

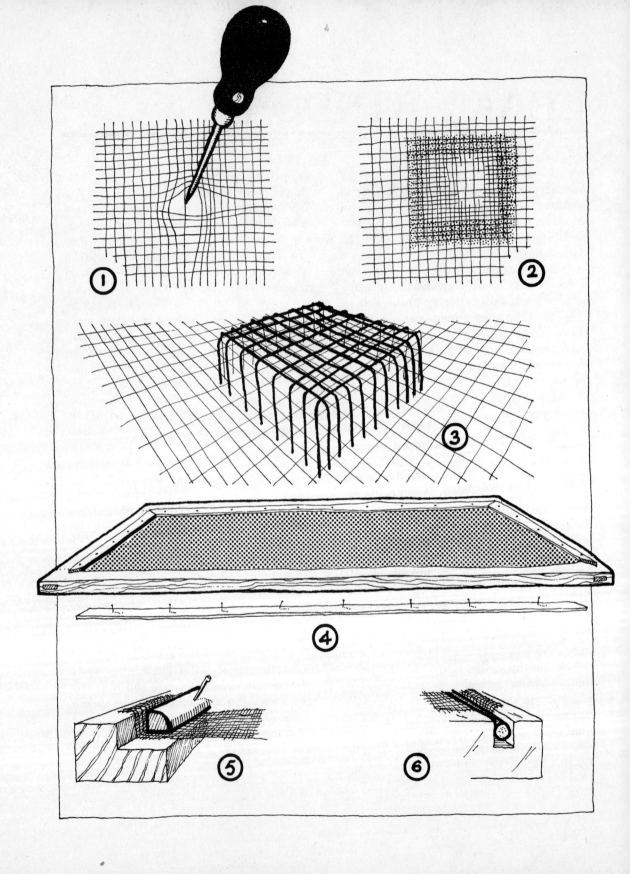

TORN SCREEN

In many areas screens are as important as storm windows and storm doors, and indeed are often used to enclose whole porches. Since they are rather delicate, damage is almost inevitable, and a single hole can destroy the usefulness of the screen. Repair is not difficult; the method depends on the size of the damage.

What sometimes appears to be a hole is often only a parting of the wires that constitute the fine mesh of a screen. Examine the hole carefully, and if you can see no broken ends all you have to do is to realign the wires with the aid of something long and thin, such as a pencil point or a small nail, or more elegantly with a scratch awl ①.

Some screens, however, are not made of wire, but of plastic. The poking and realigning method will not work for these screens and you will have to patch. For small holes or tears a slightly larger piece of screen can be glued in place. (This method will also work for wire screens.) First paint the edge of the damaged area using a clear shellac. Cut a piece of spare screen an inch larger all around than the damaged area. Then place the patch over the damaged screen and paint that part of the patch which actually overlaps the original screen. The shellac will seep through the mesh and when it dries will bond the two pieces together ②. You can also use an epoxy resin instead of shellac (especially with plastic screens).

Unless you are repairing a rip or a tear, it may look neater if you first cut the damaged area square. If the hole is of any size, in fact, you *must* cut it square because the method to use here is the woven patch method. This consists of first trimming the damage to a square hole, and then cutting a patch at least four strands larger all round than the hole, removing these outside four strands, bending them over and poking them through the screen before finally weaving them into the strands of the original screen ③.

More serious damage calls for replacement of the whole screen, which you may want to do no matter how small the damage is since patches, even very neat patches, may not look all that nice. First remove the old screen. This is usually attached by a flat strip ④, quarter-round molding in a rebate ⑤, or a neoprene strip in a special channel ⑥. (Neoprene is usually found on metal screen-frames.) In all cases remove the molding or stripping holding the screen and clean away any remaining nails, tacks, or staples that may have been used to hold the screen in place. Now cut a piece of screening as big as the entire frame. This will give you a safe working margin. Carefully align the mesh of the screen with one side of the frame (the longest side is the easiest) and secure one end of the screen to the frame—by lightly tacking or stapling if it is a wooden frame, or by inserting the neoprene strip in its channel if it is a metal frame.

For a neat job you should now similarly secure the opposite end of the screen, taking care to stretch it taut, but at the same time keeping it even. With metal frames the insertion of the neoprene strip completes the job, save for trimming the excess screen with an old knife. In the case of wooden frames it is now time to replace the molding, whether it is a surface strip or a quarter-round. Once again, work from end to end rather than proceeding around the circumference; this makes it easier to keep the screen taut. Lastly, trim off any excess screening—but try not to cut into the wood!

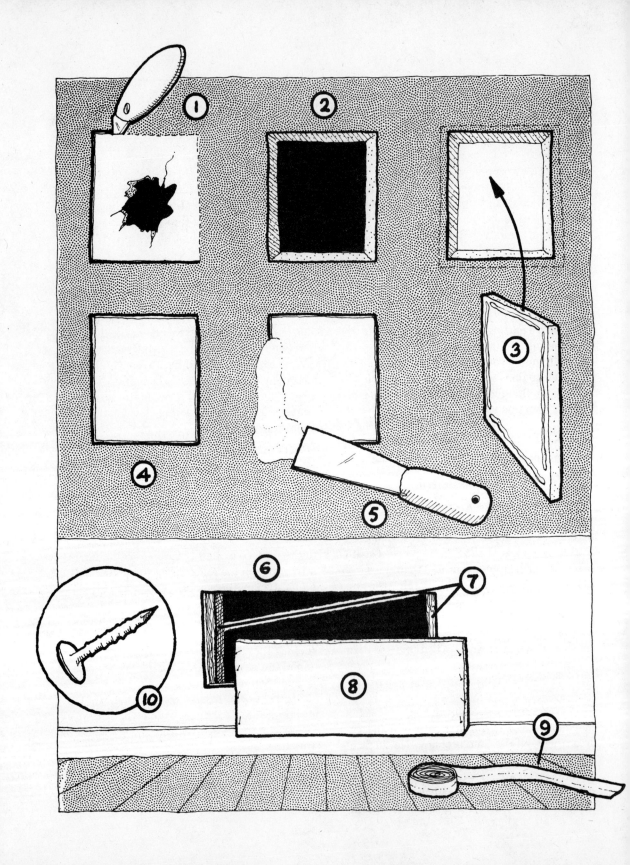

DAMAGED PLASTERBOARD

Plasterboard, also called sheetrock or gypsum board, can suffer cracks, dents, and actual holes. Repair is simple but you must have patience; the whole process sometimes takes up to three days!

Cracks or gouges must first be cleaned of any frayed paper or loose bits of material around the edges. Use a sharp utility or razor knife for this job. Anything less than a very sharp knife will simply tear the plasterboard more. Dents need no preparation. The damage may now be filled with spackle or joint compound. Do not attempt to fill the area completely level, for this first application will shrink as it dries. When it is *completely* dry—and to be sure, allow twenty-four hours—apply a second coat with a small trowel or putty knife. If there is still a depression after this second coat, give it a third coat. Finally, sand smooth and repaint.

Small holes ① should be cut square with mitered edges ②. Cut a backing piece ③ somewhat larger than the hole, coat its edges with glue, and slip it into the hole sideways. Hold it in place with a screw inserted in its face for a couple of minutes. Wait at least twenty-four hours for the glue to really harden. Then cut another piece of plasterboard, the same thickness as the damaged plasterboard, to fit as neatly as possible in the hole ④. The edges don't have to fit perfectly, but they should be mitered at approximately the same angle as the edges of the hole. Glue this piece in place. Now coat the entire patch with spackle ⑤ (or joint compound) using as

broad a knife as possible so as to obtain the flattest and levelest surface possible. Let this dry at least a couple of days. As this dries it will shrink a little and small cracks may appear in the surface. If the spackle is higher than the surrounding plasterboard sand it down lightly and then apply another coat. Repeat this process as many times as necessary.

Note that before you paint such a patch it is advisable to apply a coat of primer first, since the spackle is very absorbent and will soak up much of the paint.

For more extensive damage cut away a rectangular portion of the plasterboard ⑥ surrounding the damage large enough to expose a part of the stud on each side of the hole. These studs ⑦ are generally 16 inches apart.

Cut a new piece ⑧ to fit the hole and nail it to the exposed studs. Cover the joint with spackle (or joint compound) and lay in plasterboard tape ⑨. Cover the whole with more spackle and then gently scrape it all smooth with a broad putty knife, let it dry, and lightly sand. Apply more spackle, and sand as necessary. A few points to remember are: hammer the nails (you should use special ringed and blued sheetrock nails ⑩ which hold better and do not get rusty) below the surface, but without breaking the paper covering on the plasterboard; nail every 8 inches or so, but if you bend the nail or break the paper, set another nail a couple of inches away; use plasterboard of the same thickness as the original; and apply the spackle as smoothly as possible.

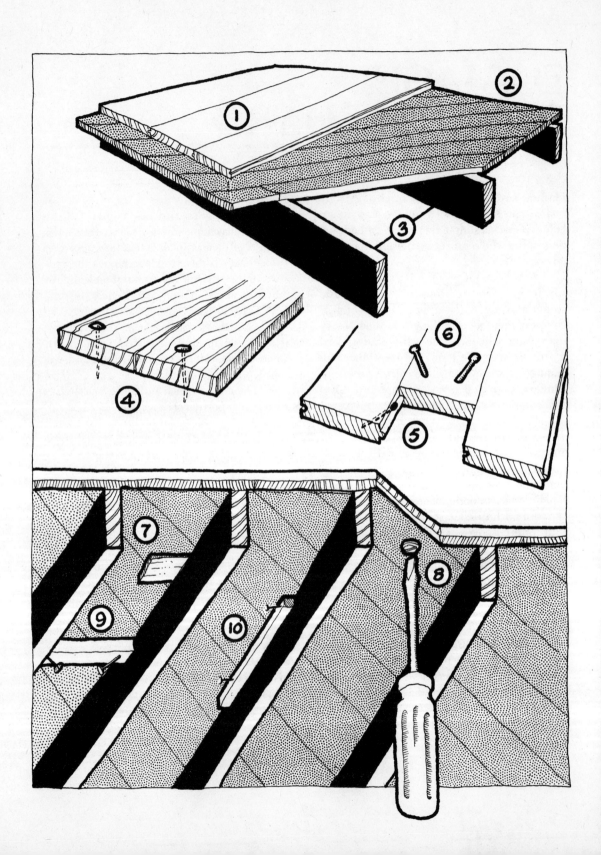

SQUEAKY FLOORS

A squeaky floor is not exactly an emergency, but it is very likely to become a nuisance which suddenly you can stand no longer, and must do something about immediately or go instantly berserk.

Before you start hammering or screwing, try something very simple: apply some powdered graphite to the cracks between the boards that seem to be sqeaking. Walk backwards and forwards over the offending area a few times, in order to give the graphite a chance to work its way in, and you may have solved the problem.

Squeaks are caused by two pieces of wood rubbing against one another. Most floors consist of two layers: a finish floor ① and a subfloor ②. The squeak may be in either or between both, or between the subfloor and the joists ③ that support it.

If the squeak is in the finish floor you must make sure that all of its boards are nailed tightly down. If it is surface-nailed you will be able to see the nail heads ③. Make sure these nails are all driven in firmly, using a hammer and a nail set (a short steel rod) in order not to mar the floor. However, most finish floors are blind-nailed ⑤ and there are no nail heads to be seen at the surface. In this case find the boards that squeak, or that seems to be loose, and drive in two nails per board at opposing angles ⑥. If it is a hardwood floor it will be easier to do this if you drill a pilot hole first, and then finish the nailing with a nail set. Without the pilot holes you might either bend the nails or split the wood. When the nails have been set a little below the surface, fill the resulting holes with matching plastic wood.

If the squeak is in the subfloor, or between the subfloor and the joists, there are several ways to silence it. First, you can drive wedges (made from wooden shingles) between the joists and the subfloor ⑦ just hard enough to stop any play between the two—but not hard enough to force the whole floor up!

Second, you can screw up through the subfloor into the finish floor and thus pull the two tightly together ⑧. To do this first drill a pilot hole just a little larger than the size screw you plan to use, through the subfloor. Then slip a washer over the screw before inserting it through the subfloor and starting to screw into the finish floor. Make sure that the screw is not long enough to stick up through the finish floor!

Third, you can nail a block under the subfloor between two adjacent joists ⑨. Toe-nailing this block from the underneath, up into the joists, will force the block upwards against the subfloor, hopefully eliminating any squeak-producing gap between the two. To ascertain exactly where this play may be, it helps to have someone walk about on top of the floor while you watch for play underneath.

One last method is to nail a ledger ⑩ along the top edge of a joist above which the subfloor seems to be loose. While nailing the ledger, push upwards so that it is pressed firmly against the subfloor—but be sure that no one is standing above this spot when you nail.

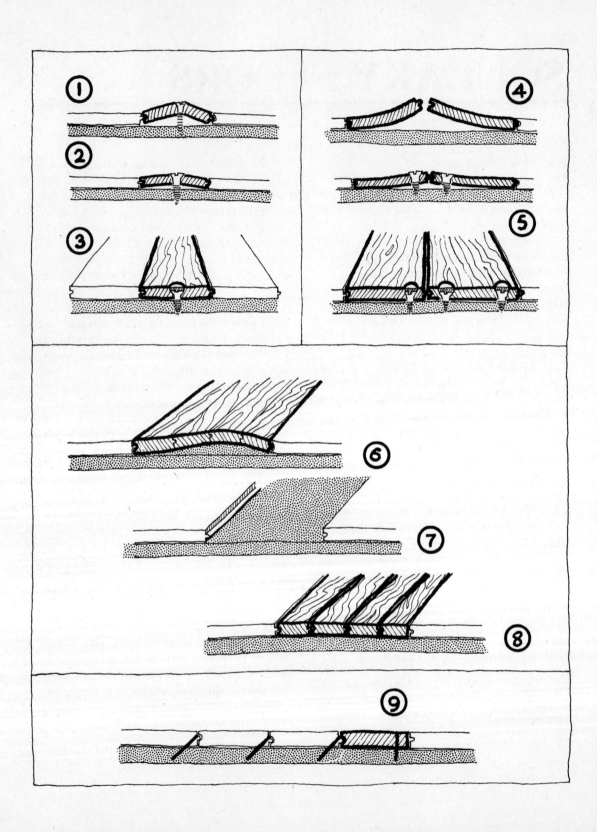

BUCKLED FLOOR

Several things can cause part of the floor to buckle, and one or more boards may be involved, but an uneven floor represents a hazard, and should be rectified as soon as possible.

One cause is a leak, from the roof or the plumbing or some other kind of accident. Too much water will cause the wood to swell and, since they can't move sideways or downwards, the board or boards involved will buckle upwards. If this is the case, lay some heavy weights on the affected part and dry the floor. Just drying without the weights may leave the wood dried in its new buckled shape. Also, the drying should be accomplished gradually. Do not wave a torch over the area—just mop up any standing water, and make sure that no more moisture reaches the spot. Leave the heat on in winter, or see that the area is well ventilated in the summer.

If the buckled area is already dry and there is visible space on either side of the board, scrape off any wax or other finish and screw the board with a countersunk screw into the subfloor ①—but do not attempt to pull the board flat immediately! Rather, cover the board with a damp rag and keep it moist for forty-eight hours. Then tighten the screw a little bit every day ② until the board is flat again. When the board is finally flat, you may plug the screw hole, either with a wooden plug the same size as the screwhead or with wood putty or plastic wood ③, and then refinish the repaired area.

The method just described works well if boards have warped in the center of their width. If adjacent boards have both curled up at their edges, and if you are sure there is enough space between them so that they will be able to lie flat again, proceed as above but with this difference: screw along the raised edges of the boards ④, but watch that the flat outer edges do not pop up as you screw down the raised sides. If it appears that this is about to happen, keep the board moist and proceed more slowly. If necessary, use screws to keep the flat side down ⑤.

For an area which is buckled and dry, but swollen so much that it is obvious the raised boards will never fit back into the space they once occupied ⑥, do not use force—you will only bruise and damage the wood further. Part of the floor must be removed ⑦ so that the wood that expanded can be reduced in size to fit. If the floor is comprised of narrow tongue-and-groove boards, the removal of one piece may be sufficient to enable the rest to be nailed down flat again. The resulting gap can be filled by sawing the removed piece into the narrower width and then fitting it back into place ⑧. This kind of flooring is usually secured by nails that go through the tongue. When you are prying boards loose work as close as possible to the nails and you will run less risk of splitting the wood. When renailing, predrilling may help. The last board or two (when you can no longer nail through the tongue) may be face nailed ⑨, using a nail set to set the nail below the surface and filling the resulting holes with plastic wood.

Another solution which works better with wider boards is to get below the floor, if this is possible, and screw up through the subfloor into the warped board, thereby pulling it down flat. The only thing to be careful about here is that you do not screw all the way through; choose a screw of appropriate length.

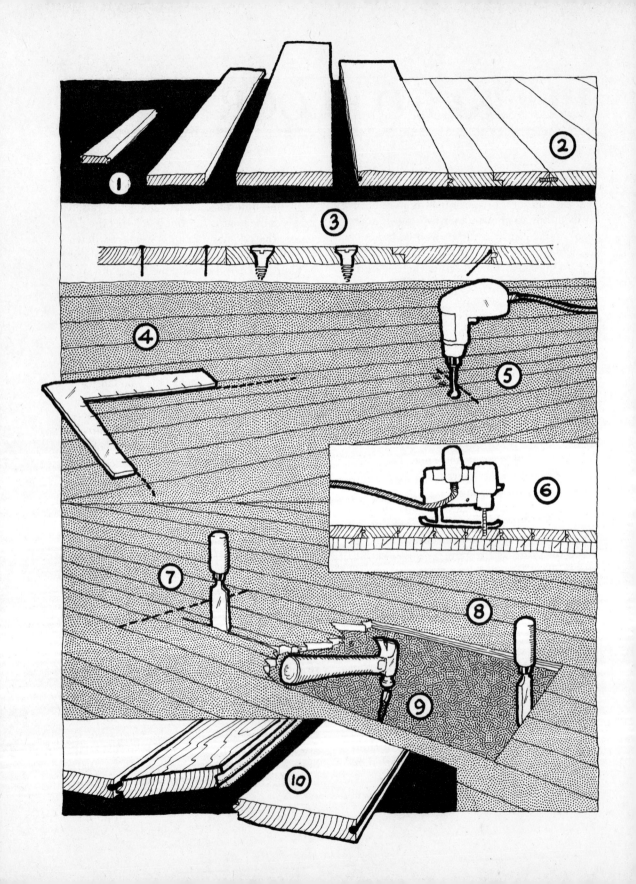

HOLE IN FLOOR

The movers drop the piano, a weakened board suddenly gives way, a small fire burns a hole, or some other accident necessitates the removal and replacement of part of the floor—this section shows how this repair is done.

Wooden floors are most commonly laid over a subfloor. In older buildings this usually consists of floorboards laid diagonally across the joists (see ② page 21), and in more modern buildings generally consists of plywood sheeting. This is important to bear in mind because if you are going to cut or saw out a section of damaged floor you must be careful not to damage the subfloor at the same time.

There is great variation in the width of floorboards, from 2-inch by 6-inch strips of parquet flooring, to 16-inch-wide pine planks, with everything else in between ①. However, almost all floorboards are joined at their edges by some form of groove ②. Furthermore, if you can't see the nails (or plugged screws) holding the boards down, the chances are that the boards are blind-nailed through these grooves ③.

Now, bearing the above in mind, draw a line, using a carpenter's framing square held at right angles to the ends of the damaged board or boards ④. This marks off the area to be removed—large or small, as the case may be.

If you are removing just one or two narrow boards there may not be room enough to use a saw, so drill a series of small holes just inside the line enclosing the damaged area ⑤. You may not know how thick the board is, so drill slowly and, bearing in mind that most flooring is between ⅝ inch and 1½ inches thick, stop when you feel a difference in the resistance to the drill within these measurements. To be safe, wrap a piece of tape around

the drill bit 1 inch from its end. This will act as a depth guide. Remember that there may be hidden nails near the edges of boards; do not go too close. If you can see wooden plugs, chisel them out to reveal the screws and remove the screws with a screwdriver.

If the section to be removed is wide enough, you can saw instead of drilling. Use a circular saw (electric) with a depth gauge. Set the gauge to ½ inch, and saw just inside your line ⑥. If this does not cut all the way through, increase the depth gauge setting in ⅛-inch increments until it does. When the ends of the area are cut, the easiest thing to do it to split out the middle using a plastic-handled chisel ⑦. This should remove most of the wood and you can now clean up the ends with the chisel ⑧. The sides may be a little more difficult because of the grooves mentioned earlier. Using a nail set, drive all the nails you can see right through the board into the subfloor ⑨, so that they are no longer holding the finish floor. Now you should be able to remove the remainder of the old boards.

Fitting new boards is mainly a matter of exact measuring and careful sawing. You will, of course, use wood that is the same thickness. If you are replacing several boards you will be able to blind-nail all but the last, and face-nailing followed by setting of the nails and filling of the nail holes is quite acceptable. The only difficulty arises from the tongue-and-groove at the edges. This is dealt with by inserting the boards tongue first and removing the bottom of the last board's groove ⑩. Alternatively, if the replacement boards are not tongue-and-grooved, remove the tongue of the existing floorboard and insert square-edged boards.

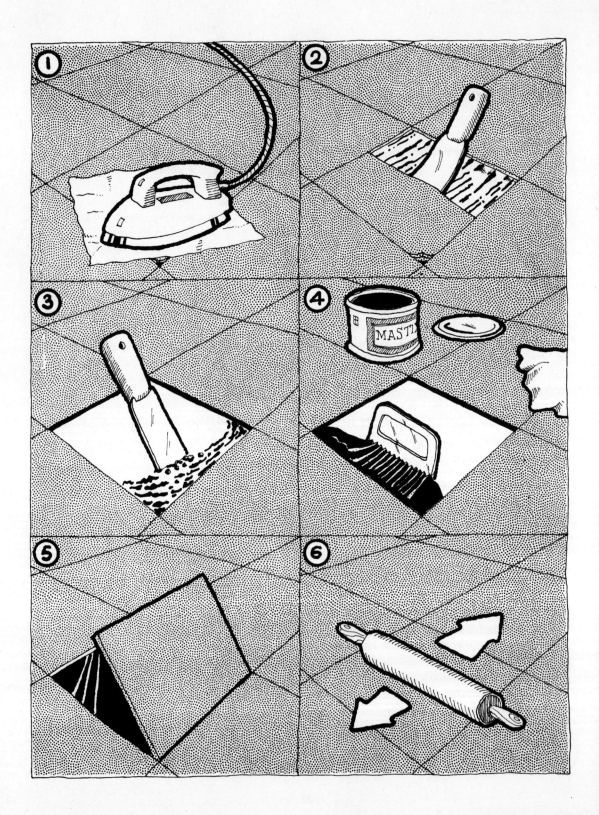

DAMAGED FLOOR TILE

Resilient floor coverings may be in either sheet form or tile form, and may be made from a variety of materials such as cork, rubber, asphalt, vinyl-asbestos, or linoleum. Damage can range from stains and scratches to gouges requiring the replacement of that section.

Stains or marks can be best removed by using household bleach, ammonia and water, lighter fluid (but be careful), white vinegar, or even rubbing alcohol. Always experiment in an inconspicuous corner first to make sure that you do not damage the hard finish—be wary of chemical cleaners for the same reason.

Scratches or gouges can sometimes be masked by making a fine powder of a matching tile and then mixing it to a thick paste with acetone, smoothing the paste over the blemish and, when dry, finishing with fine wire wool.

Curled edges should be heated by ironing them through a sheet of aluminum foil until they are pliable ①. The mastic that originally held them in place must be scraped away and new adhesive applied. Excess mastic should be wiped up, and the reglued corner weighted down at least overnight.

To replace a whole tile you must first completely remove the old one. The most important thing is not to damage the edges of the adjoining tiles. Heat the tile a little with a household iron first ①. When it becomes soft, try slipping a putty knife under the edge and working across to the other side. If you are in any danger of damaging adjacent tiles,

make a cut in the middle of the damaged tile, force your putty knife in, and work outwards to the edges ②.

Once again it is important to clean away all the old glue or mastic and other debris ③. Before applying any new adhesive, first make sure that the replacement tile will fit as perfectly as possible in the space. Sand away any excess. It is also important to use the correct adhesive for the kind of tile you are laying. Make sure of this at the tile supplier; mismatched tile and adhesive can be a disaster.

Use a serrated spreader and follow the manufacturer's directions when applying the adhesive to the exposed work area ④. Be extremely careful not to get any adhesive where it is not required. In the event that you do, have a damp cloth ready to remove any mistakes.

Here is a very valuable tip: place the new tile in position by setting one edge of it against one of the exposed edges of the surrounding tiles ⑤. Do not attempt to slide it into place or it may well stick fast before you have it in position. At the least you will simply scrape up and squeeze out adhesive along the joints.

Softer tiles, like rubber or linoleum, can now be rolled firmly down using a rolling pin ⑥. Wipe up any oozed adhesive and weight the tile down overnight. Lastly, wait a few days before applying any finish, such as wax or polish, and before mopping the area.

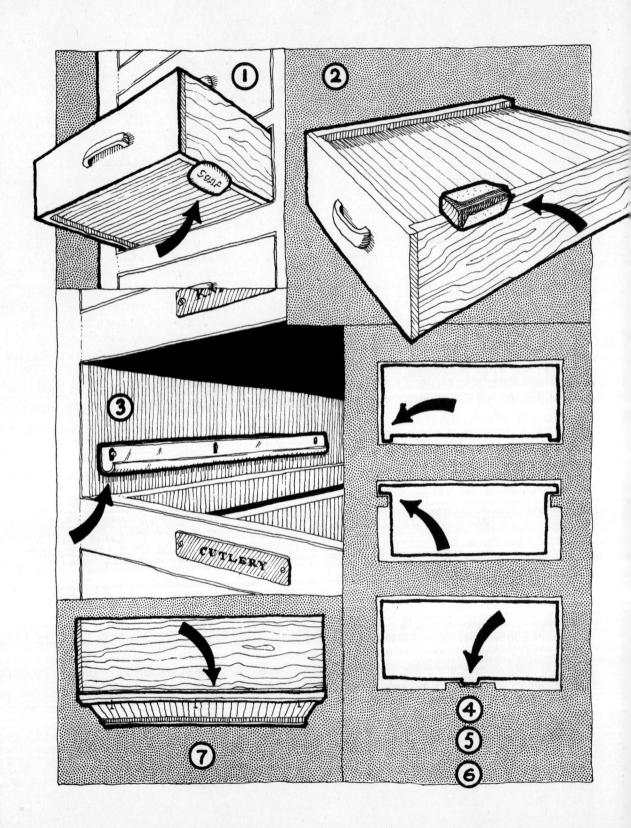

JAMMED DRAWERS

Drawers that receive a lot of use, especially the softwood kind frequently used in kitchen cabinetry, wear remarkably quickly and can suffer all kinds of irritating defects, many of which manifest themselves by causing the drawer to jam.

If possible, try to gain access to the jammed drawer through an adjacent drawer which you can remove, or through a cupboard or other space. Attempt to jiggle the offending drawer into perfect alignment before trying to push it out. Push, rather than pull, in order to avoid the possibility of pulling the front off, leaving the rest of the drawer still stuck!

If the drawer jammed simply because it was stuffed too full, and some of the contents caught in the casing, the cure is obvious—put less in it. Otherwise, remove the drawer completely for analysis. It will have stuck for one of two opposite reasons: either it was too big for the space it occupied, or it was too small. Being too big can be caused by swelling as a result of moisture absorption, or by a part having warped out of shape (which can also be caused by moisture), or often by part of the drawer having become loose. Remove the cause of the moisture, let the drawer dry out, completely glue any loose pieces back together again, and then try it for fit. If it is still difficult to slide in and out, and there is no hardware such as metal runners ③ involved, try lubricating the wooden parts which rub against the case with paraffin wax or even household soap ①. This can often work wonders. If still sticky, look for shiny spots on the drawer bottom and sides. These show where the drawer is rubbing. You should sand these spots lightly with fine sandpaper until the whole thing slides smoothly again ②.

If the drawer runs on metal slides these may be causing the problem. First of all check that the hardware has not worked loose. Make sure all holding screws ③ are tight and nothing wobbles about. Clean out any dirt or debris that may have crept into the works. Matchsticks and hairpins are common culprits. Apply a little lubricant to all moving parts and all parts that slide against one another. Check for alignment—if a runner guide is not perfectly parallel with the rest of the fitting it can bind. Most runners are secured to the woodwork by screws inserted through slots which allow a certain amount of adjustments.

Drawers without sliding hardware that wear with use can jam because they become smaller than originally built, and the extra play allowed by the wear then causes trouble.

The most common wear occurs under the sides ④, which is where many drawers slide. Some drawers slide on arms positioned on the sides of the case ⑤. Still other drawers may run on a wooden rail centrally situated underneath the drawer ⑥. Wherever the wear takes place it is usually readily apparent on inspection. Depending on how the drawer and its case were put together, you may be able to simply replace the sliding parts. Many slides are just nailed into the sides of the case. If this is the situation, then just pry them off and make new ones to the original size and renail ⑦. If it is the bottom of the drawer that has worn, or even broken, you can try laminating an extra piece on.

One last thing to be aware of is that it is also possible for drawers to stick because the whole enclosure has tilted, perhaps due to settling of the house. If this is the case then you must try to realign the case, perhaps with shims under one side or the other.

ROOF LEAK

Roof leaks are among the worst kind of household emergency since repair is almost always done from the outside, and the leak is generally only noticed in inclement weather. The usual course of action is to rush about with pots and pans, trying to mop up and catch the leaks ①, and then quit until the weather improves. The first part of this procedure is all right, but the second part will not help any eventual repair, since the best time to locate the source of many leaks is while it is still raining. If you wait until everything has dried up you might look forever for the source of that drip.

 If you can gain access to the underside of the roof, from the attic, for instance, look first for the spot where the water is going through the ceiling ②. The point of entry is rarely directly over the dripping, but mark this area anyway—it will provide you with a starting point later. Then try and follow the drip, or wetness, to what appears to be its source ③. Look for water stains on rafters; if it's daytime look for pinpricks of light in the roof; look most carefully around anything that goes through the roof, such as a chimney stack or a vent pipe; and pay special attention to places where two roof slopes meet, such as valleys, dormers, and ridges. When you think you have found the source, mark it with chalk or crayon.

 Finding the source may be all you can do at this point. If the leak is so disastrous as to require some immediate remedy, you may have to brave the elements and staple, tack, or even nail a sheet of plastic or building paper over the damage; but weigh the risk of venturing onto a wet and possibly windy roof against the potential water damage very carefully.

 If you do decide to do more before calling a professional roofer, the next thing to do is to get up on the roof (when conditions have improved) and look for the source of the problem. If you think you have found it from the inside, the way to locate that spot on the outside is by driving a thin nail up through the roof from the spot you marked inside ④. The most likely places for leaks to develop are where asphalt or wood shingles appear cracked or worn, or where slate and tile is broken, or even missing. Look carefully at all the places where there is flashing—the metal seams around things that protrude through the roof—such as chimneys ⑤, where different roof slopes meet ⑤, or where skylights exist.

 Small leaks such as you might find in and around flashed areas can be fixed with a liberal application of roofing tar, or sometimes more neatly with caulk squeezed out with the help of a caulking gun.

 Torn, cracked, or missing shingles can often be made leak-proof by sliding a piece of flashing up underneath, nailing it in place, and then covering the nail holes and the edges of the flashing with roofing tar. Force the flashing up with a block of wood as shown ⑥. You may need to do this on several adjacent courses.

 Repairs involving more than applications of roofing tar can become complicated, and are probably best left to a professional (as are any repairs where you see that the shingles are excessively worn, cracked, lacking their gravel coating, or if wooden, covered in moss, or split). Asphalt and wood shingles do not last forever, and deterioration and replacement is eventually unavoidable. Slate and tile on the other hand, while initially considerably more expensive, will last much longer.

GUTTER PROBLEMS

Gutters, which are designed to carry away the water which runs off the roof, are quite simple. There is not much that can go wrong with them besides blockages, leaks, and complete or partial collapse. Replacement at lengthy intervals is generally the rule, but if a leak should develop right over your entrance door, you might want to attend to it right away.

The key to trouble-free gutters is regular cleaning. It doesn't have to be done often, perhaps twice a year will suffice—once right after all the leaves have fallen and once again six months later. If your gutters have not been cleaned in a while, then that is the first thing to do when trouble strikes. You can't fix a leak in a gutter clogged with debris, and you may even find that what you thought was a leak is simply water spilling over because its progress has been blocked ①.

Gutters should slope gently over their entire length to a low point where the leader or downspout is connected ②. At this junction a wire basket or strainer ③ is often installed to catch leaves and other debris and prevent it all from being washed into the downspout ④. Make sure this is clean, and equally important, make sure it has not rusted away to worthlessness. If it has, buy a replacement at the hardware store. If there was no strainer to begin with, make sure the downspout is clear before you start cleaning the gutter. Do this by pouring a little water into the top and seeing if it comes out the bottom. If it doesn't, try cleaning it out with a wire coat hanger. In very many cases the downspout makes some turns immediately below the gutter in order to hug the building more closely. It is in these turns that you are most likely to find the blockage. If not, then probably the easiest thing to do is to disassemble the down-

spout into its constituent lengths. These may be simply pushed together and held in place by virtue of the fasteners that hold the whole thing to the wall ⑤, or they may be held together with sheet metal screws that can be easily removed.

When you are sure that the downspout is in good working order, complete with wire strainer, it is time to clean the gutter. Start at the high end and, using a hose and a putty knife, loosen the debris and wash it down the gutter.

If the cleaning has revealed extensive rust and holes, the only satisfactory remedy is to replace the gutter. If the leak is small it can be temporarily patched with a piece of building paper or asphalt roofing paper ⑥ liberally coated with roofing tar (which you can buy in a can or in a cartridge for use with a caulking gun).

The life of the gutter can be lengthened considerably by keeping it clean and painting it with metal paint, but try and start out with a good grade of galvanized metal if you buy new guttering.

The other main problem that can beset gutters is trouble with the attached fittings. There are many ways that gutters are attached (sometimes they are even built right into the roof itself), but whatever system your gutters use—straps, flanges, or brackets—make sure that all nails or screws are tight, and replace any fitting that has broken. Bear in mind that you *must* ensure a continuous slope, or standing water will appear and hasten the advent of rust. Also note that gutters should not present a barrier to any snow that may slide off the roof. This means that they must be set back behind an imaginary line continuing the slope of the roof ⑦.

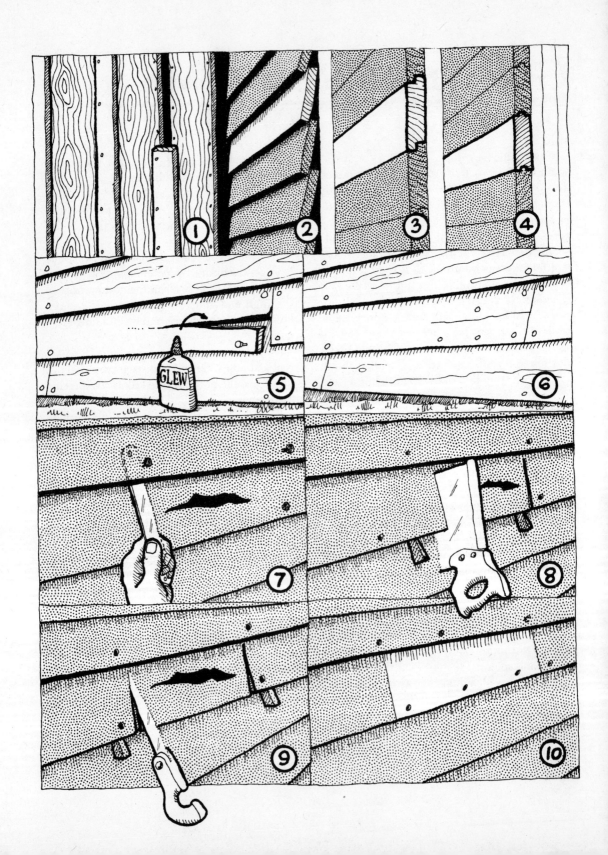

DAMAGED SIDING

There are many varieties of siding, which is the exterior wooden wall covering. The easiest to repair is board and batten ①. The battens are easily pried off, which exposes gaps between the boards, and the boards themselves can be pried off and replaced as necessary.

Horizontal siding may be divided into innumerable variations of clapboard ②, shiplap ③, or tongue-and-groove ④. Plywood is also used for siding. In this case repair usually consists of replacing the entire damaged sheet.

Rather than replacing a damaged board, it may be possible to repair it. This is a lot quicker, so give it a try. Split boards should be pried apart so that waterproof glue can be squeezed into and behind the crack ⑤, and then nailed firmly back into place ⑥.

Warped boards can sometimes be pulled back into place with a line of screws. Try to get the screws into a stud (this can be located by looking for the vertical line of nails often visible in siding), and do not insert them too closely together—or the board may split.

A small hole, such as one caused by a knot falling out, should be plugged with oakum (available at hardware stores or plumbing supply houses) and then caulked and painted.

If the board (or boards) is beyond repair and must be replaced, follow this method. First, in the case of all varieties of clapboard, remove the visible nails either by prying the board out a little until the nail head pops out sufficiently to enable you to get a nail puller under it, or by sliding a hacksaw blade up under the board ⑦. The damaged section should now be wedged out a little from the rest of the siding and sawed free, first using a backsaw ⑧, and then (for the part that may remain stuck under the board above) a keyhole saw ⑨. A new section (of the same size and type) can now be slid into place and securely nailed ⑩. When sliding the new piece into place, resist the temptation to whack it in with a hammer and use a scrap of wood for this purpose—it will save the edge and distribute the force more evenly.

Shiplap siding is hard to pry loose in the above manner. The best course of action is to set a circular saw to the same thickness as the siding, saw up both sides of the damaged section, and then along the middle (in order to miss any hidden nails). Now you can remove it with a hammer and chisel. The nails must be removed with a nail remover or a hacksaw. If there is any damage to the building paper that usually lines the building beneath the siding then this must also be patched or caulked. Replacing a new section is easy, but take care to get the closest possible fit when measuring. Any gaps left when the board is in place should be filled and sanded, and then painted over.

The procedure for repairing damaged tongue-and-groove siding is necessarily the same as for shiplap, since visual inspection alone may not offer you any clues as to which type you have.

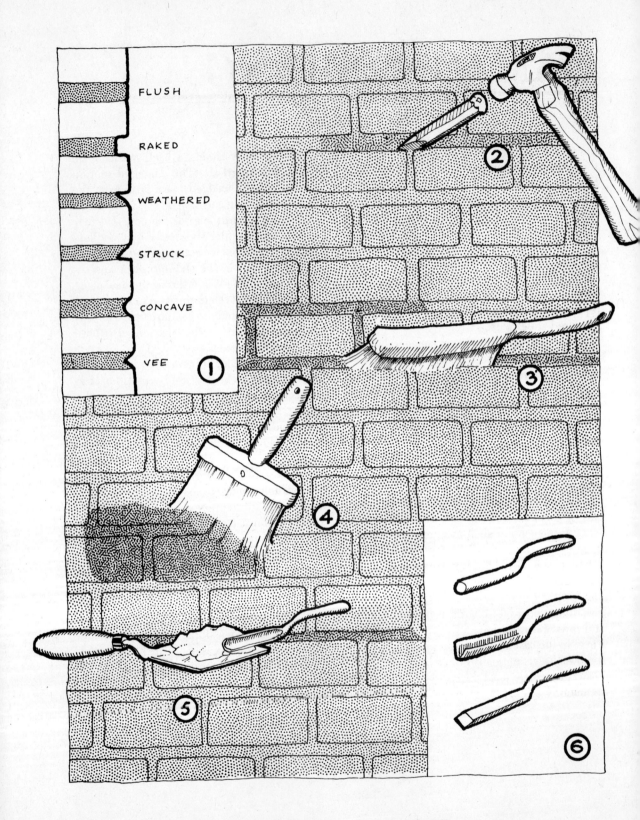

FLUSH

RAKED

WEATHERED

STRUCK

CONCAVE

VEE

①

②

③

④

⑤

⑥

CRUMBLING
BRICKWORK JOINTS

If the actual bricks in chimneys, walls, or foundations show signs of serious deterioration, it is time to call in the mason. If it is just the mortar in the joints that suddenly strikes you as being in danger of crumbling away, you can probably take care of the repairs yourself. Needless to say, if the whole expanse is in a similar condition it will be more economical to have it "pointed"—the technical term for repairing crumbly mortar—by a professional who will have all sorts of equipment on hand, such as scaffolding, cement mixers, etc.

The way the joints between brickwork are finished off—the proper term is "struck"—varies according to taste and more importantly according to the climate ①. So while you should finish your repairs in the same style as the existing brickwork, it would be foolish, in a temperate region, to use a struck joint that is more suited to a hot climate. If your repair area is relatively small, it is probably not very important, but if a large area is involved, you would be well advised to consult a mason about the appropriateness of your style of pointing.

Mortar crumbles partly because of inferior materials and shoddy mixing, and partly because extreme winter temperatures freeze moisture that has penetrated the joints. The first thing to do is to clean out all of the crumbled mortar using a cold chisel ② to chip away about ½ inch of the joint and then a wire brush ③ to remove the particles.

After having cleaned away all the loose mortar, wet the area thoroughly ④. This is to stop the dry brickwork from absorbing the moisture in the new mortar and causing it to dry too quickly—thereby losing its strength. Next, mix the mortar. The correct proportions are one part masonry cement to three parts fine sand. Mix the cement and sand thoroughly, and *then* add water, slowly. A little stiffer than a good waffle mix is an ideal consistency. It must be smooth and should stick to the trowel for a while when you hold the trowel upside down. Alternatively, you can buy premixed mortar cement in small quantities from building supply or hardware stores.

Take a small trowel, put some mortar on it, and push the mortar off the trowel into the joint, holding the trowel very close to the wall ⑤. The pusher should be a striking tool which matches the joints in your brickwork. These tools are very inexpensive and will ensure that you get the mortar right into the joint and can finish it off to look nice and smooth.

If an area of brickwork cracks, it could be either slight settling or a more serious problem with the foundation. One way to find out is as follows. Using an epoxy or other strong waterproof glue, stick a piece of glass across the crack. If after a while (several weeks, or several months if you want to be really sure) the glass is still in place, then it is probably just a minor crack that is worth repairing in the same manner as described above. But if the glass has pulled off or pulled apart, then you have a more serious problem and should call in a builder or mason to check the foundations.

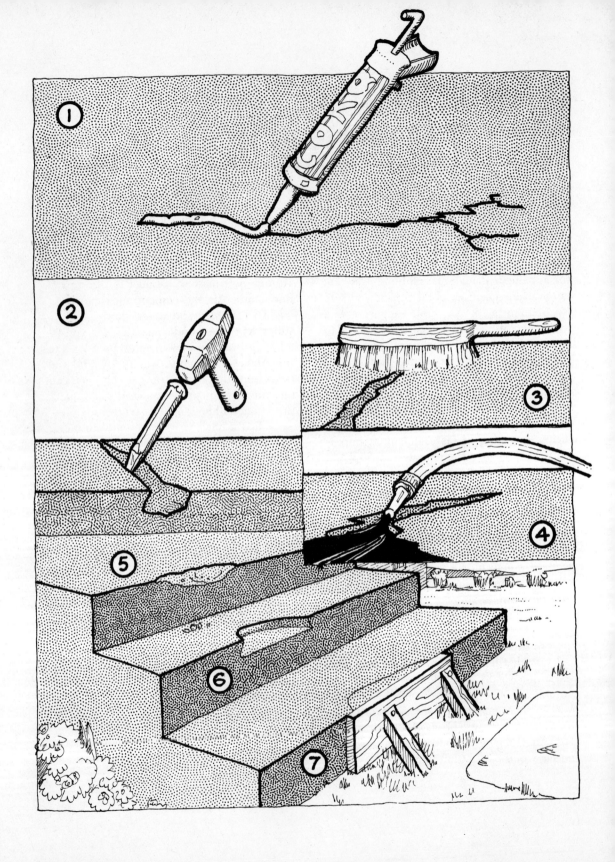

BROKEN CONCRETE

Concrete appears in many places around the home, from paths and steps to walls and floors. Although it seems hard and durable, it is actually susceptible to a lot of damage—from cracks and chips to complete disintegration.

Small, hairline cracks are almost inevitable, but if you are determined to maintain a flawless building, then they can be brushed clean and caulked ①.

Larger cracks should definitely be repaired to prevent water from entering and then freezing—eventually splitting the concrete. They can be dealt with by first undercutting their edges with a cold chisel ②. This is done so that the patch will not fall out. When you have thoroughly cleaned the undercut crack of all loose material using a wire brush ③, soak the area thoroughly ④. If the patch is applied to a dry area, the concrete, which is very porous and absorptive, will suck the moisture out of the patching material and dry it far too quickly for it to be able to cure properly. The result will be a patch that soon crumbles and falls out. Don't go so far as to leave puddles of standing water, however.

Finally, the crack may be filled either with cement you have mixed yourself or with a commercial masonry patching material such as a latex, epoxy, vinyl, or acrylic cement that comes in a cartridge. If there is only a small amount to be done and you prefer to use cement, which is still considered the best material, you may find it more convenient to buy a premixed bag—they are available in different sizes from 10 pounds to 90 pounds. If you mix

your own cement, use one part Portland cement to three parts sand, and not so much water that the mix is sloppy but not so little that the mix is too stiff to work (if you can throw it against the wall and it sticks there, it is just right).

In any event, work the material of your choice well into the crack, removing all air bubbles, and then keep it damp by covering it with plastic and wetting it down occasionally for the first forty-eight hours. If it dries too quickly it will only crack again and you will be back where you started!

The procedure for repairing larger holes, such as the broken edges of concrete steps ⑤, is similar to the process of repairing cracks. Provide a flat landing ⑥ for the patching material by chipping away with the cold chisel. Dampen the area ④, and then fill it, providing some support ⑦ for the wet mix, which should contain some small stones (the stones are the extra ingredient that turns cement into concrete).

The support, which should be pregreased so that concrete will not stick to it when it's removed, must be very firmly held in place because wet concrete is very heavy. Just as when repairing a crack, it is of paramount importance to allow the repair to cure slowly, or it will crack. Keep it damp and covered to start with. Depending on the weather and the thickness of the new work, it can take up to a week to cure or harden completely. So if in doubt, be patient.

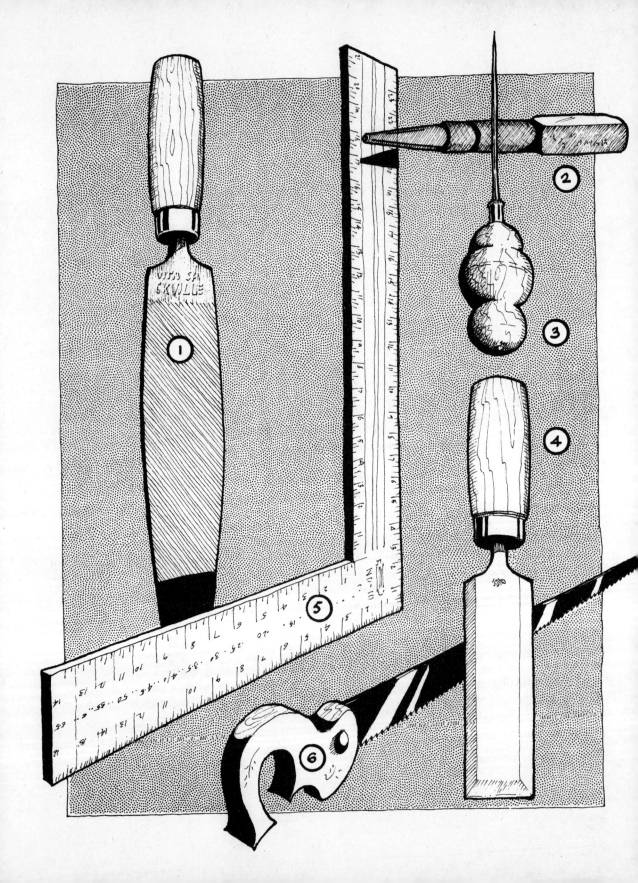

TOOLS

The following tools, although listed here at the end of Part One, may also be found useful in the other parts of this book. None of them is expensive, and all of them are simple to use if you know how. But remember, it almost never pays to buy a cheap tool, such as you might find in the "dollar bin." Not only will it do its job poorly, it won't last, and you will have wasted your dollar and caused yourself frustration and aggravation that could have been avoided by the purchase of a better quality tool. It is false logic to say "I am not a professional, therefore I do not need the best." If anything, precisely because you *are* an amateur you need all the help you can get; adding an inferior tool to your lack of experience is simply increasing your disadvantage.

A file ① is actually a cutting tool, and like all other cutting tools only works well if it is sharp. Each little groove is a cutting edge that should be protected if it is to remain effective. Therefore, do not keep your file in the bottom of your tool box or drawer where everything else will bang up against it and inevitably dull its efficiency. If kept sharp you will find it endlessly useful for taking down protruding bolts, filing the underside of sticking drawers, smoothing door bottoms, and helping screens to fit better.

The nail set ② is actually made in four sizes, but the possession and use of any one of the four sizes will add dramatically to the professional appearance of any hammering work you may have to do. When you get a nail close to the surface, instead of sinking it all the way into the wood with the hammer head—and in so doing, denting the wood—place the tip of the nail set on the head of the nail, and hammer the end of the nail set until the nail is, indeed, set!

A scratch awl ③ is simply a sharp point with a handle. You really only need one, kept sharp by a little judicious use of the file. Although its chief use in the hands of a carpenter is to mark wood to be sawn and cut, once you have one you will find that you use it for all kinds of things, from making small holes for starting screws to straightening the mesh in wire screens.

A chisel ④ is a member of one of the largest families of tools. There are dozens of different sorts, in all shapes and sizes, used by the widest possible array of woodworkers. For common household use, find one with a straight blade about an inch wide. Do *not* use it as a screwdriver (you should have several of these, anyway), and keep it sharp. Bevelled edges, handles of different materials, and many other varying features all have their specific uses, but as long as you do not let the edge become dull and knicked, any medium-sized and -shaped chisel will do sterling service around the house.

The carpenter's framing square ⑤ is a precision measuring tool, usually inscribed with so many figures, tables, and measurements that whole books have been written concerning its use. But simply having one handy will prove wonderfully useful when it comes to marking out large right-angled squares, drawing straight lines, and checking the squareness of doors, drawers, and windows. Just be careful not to step on it or it will no longer be a square!

The keyhole saw ⑥ is a small, specialized saw that you can use in many places where a regular saw is simply too large to fit. Because it is so narrow you must take care not to bend its blade—and, of course, keep it sharp.

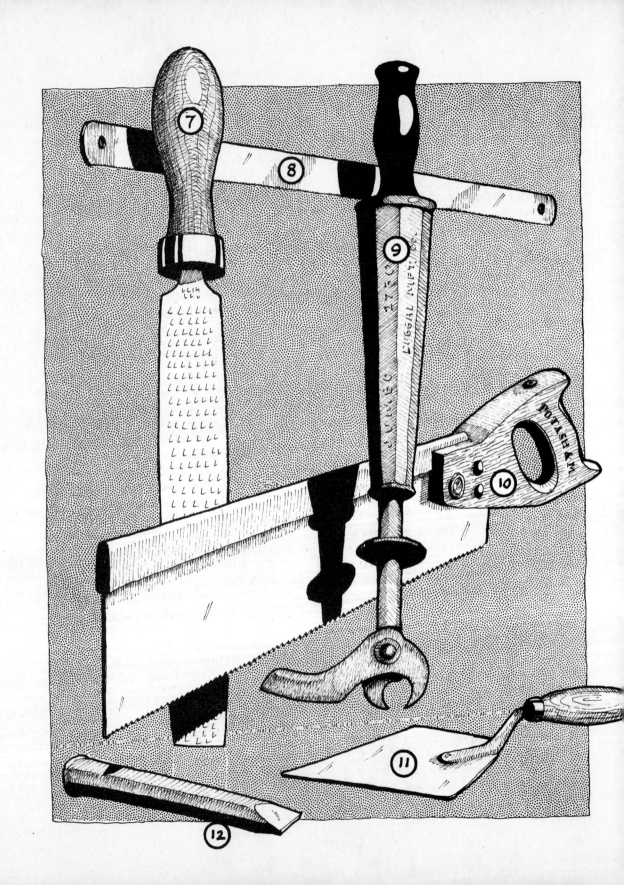

MORE TOOLS

The rasp ⑦ is similar to, and, indeed, related to the file shown on page 41. Its cutting edges are even more vulnerable, and so it should be kept where other tools cannot bang into it. Its chief use is to remove excess wood that is too much for a file or sandpaper to remove but not enough for a saw to work on. It will also shape wood into curves. It is a handy tool to have around when you are working on ill-fitting doors and windows, and also when you are trying to fit replacement pieces of wood, such as floorboards.

A hacksaw blade ⑧, with or without the frame that turns it into the complete hacksaw, is almost indispensable. You should never use a wood saw for cutting anything but wood, yet there are lots of things which can only be sawed—such as nails, pipes, and other materials—and the hacksaw is the correct tool to use.

A nail puller ⑨ is a specialized tool for which there is no substitute. If you ever have to remove large nails from anything and intend to use the nailed wood again, the nail puller is the tool to use.

A backsaw ⑩, originally called a tenon saw because one of its chief uses is to saw the tenons out of wood being made ready for mortise-and-tenon joints, is basically a medium-sized saw with a metal stiffener along its back. If the piece of wood you wish to saw is no thicker than the depth of the blade up to the stiffener, the backsaw is infinitely easier to use than the keyhole saw described previously. For a good example of its use, see page 35.

The cold chisel ⑫ and the trowel ⑪ are basically masons' tools, and their uses are exemplified on pages 37 to 39. Like many other tools, however, further uses will be discovered for them once they are in your possession.

There is an almost endless array of tools, and although you may find that with just a few you can improvise most jobs, it is always a pleasure to have the right tool for the job. How many you want to acquire will depend on your own personal feelings towards taking care of problems around the house, but you may find that they are addictive, and if this happens you will never have enough. Tools are, after all, one of the things that make us distinctively human.

PART TWO

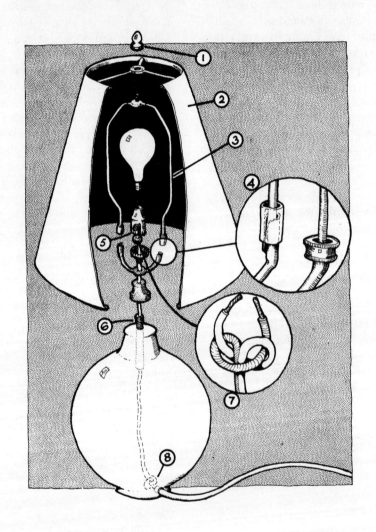

ELECTRICAL REPAIRS

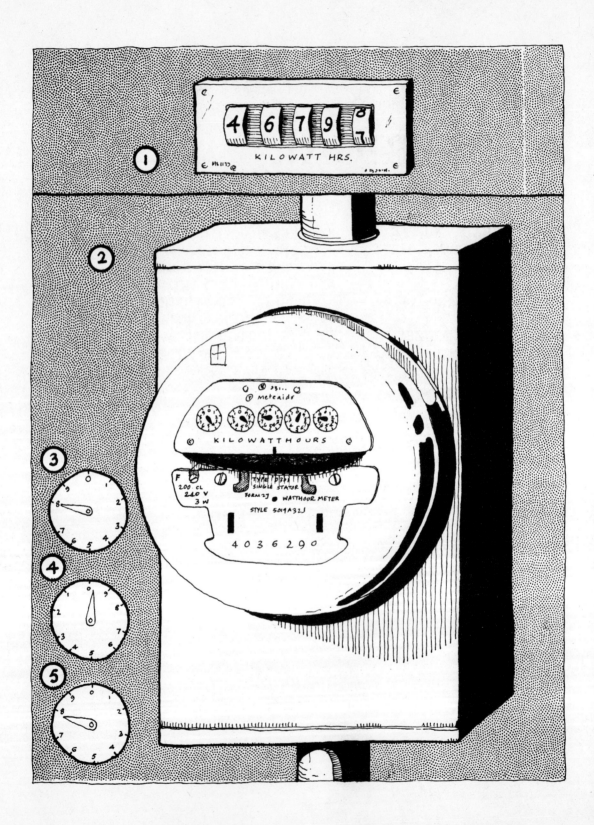

HOW TO READ A METER

If you take any interest in the running of your home it probably starts with the bills. In order to understand your electric bill it helps to be able to read the meter, because this way you can monitor your usage from month to month (or even on a shorter basis if you wish).

There are two basic types of meter commonly in use. The direct readout type shown ① is not difficult to read. Just remember that if two numbers are showing, as is the case in the last window, read the lower number. The meter in this case reads 46797.

At the end of the month (or week or day) read the meter again and the number will be higher. Subtract the first number from the new number. The result will be the number of kilowatt hours of electricity you have used. Most utility companies print their rates on their bills, and a simple multiplication of the rate by the number of kilowatt hours used will tell you how much you have to pay (less sales tax, of course).

The other type of meter is the dial type, as shown at ②. This is a little trickier to read. First, notice that instead of five windows there are five clocklike dials. Second, what is not always immediately apparent is that these dials are numbered alternately clockwise and anticlockwise! (This is the result of the gearing inside—and an example of perversity on the part of the meter makers or the utility company—which is designed to make the meter more difficult to read.)

The complete number is read from left to right, and each individual dial is read bearing the following points in mind. If, as at ③, the needle appears to be directly on a number, look at the following dial (on its right) to see if its needle has reached 0. If, as at ④, it hasn't, then the number at ③ should be read as 7. If, on the other hand, the needle at ④ is pointing directly at 0 (which is actually 10), then the number at ③ should be read as 8.

If the needle is not directly on a number, then it will be between two numbers (as at ⑤). You should always take the lower of these two numbers. But remember, as mentioned before, that 0 represents 10, and that therefore when the needle is between 0 and 9 on the dial the number to be read is 9.

Last, while doing all this, do not forget that alternate dials are numbered in different directions. The dials shown at ③, ④, and ⑤ are the last three dials of the meter at ②. The reading on this meter is therefore the same as that on the direct readout type at ①, namely 46797.

Wattages Of Appliances Used In The Home

AIR CONDITIONER	1100	HOT PLATE	1500
ATTIC FAN	400	LIGHT BULB	40–150
AUTOMATIC TOASTER	1200	MIXER	100
AUTOMATIC WASHER	700	OIL BURNER	250
BROILER	1000	PORTABLE FAN	100
BUILT-IN VENTILATING FAN	400	PORTABLE HEATER	1650
COFFEE MAKER	1000	RADIO	100
EGG COOKER	600	RANGE	8000
DEEP FRYER	1320	REFRIGERATOR	200
DEHUMIDIFIER	350	ROTISSERIE	1380
DISHWASHER	1500	ROASTER	1380
DRY IRON OR STEAM IRON	1000	SANDWICH GRILL	1320
ELECTRIC BLANKET	200	TELEVISION	500
ELECTRIC CLOCK	2	VACUUM CLEANER	300
CLOTHES DRYER	4500	VENTILATING FAN	400
FREEZER	350	WAFFLE IRON	1320
FLUORESCENT LIGHT	15–40	WASTE DISPOSER	500
GRIDDLE	1000	WATER HEATER	2500
HAIR DRYER	100	WATER PUMP	700
HEAT OR SUN LAMP	300		

WHERE THE
ELECTRICITY GOES

Your electrical system begins at the meter described in the previous section and then proceeds to the service box described on page 51. From this point it runs in a number of circuits throughout your home.

Many problems which might be blamed on the various appliances fed by this electricity can often be traced to inadequate wiring. Besides not getting full efficiency from appliances, overloaded wires can heat up and waste the current you pay for. If improperly fused they can create a dangerous fire hazard. If you are experiencing any of the following problems you probably need professional help in improving the wiring of your house:

1. Lights dim when appliances are turned on.
2. Toasters, heaters, and irons heat up too slowly.
3. Television picture shrinks in size when appliances are turned on.
4. Many appliances are plugged into the same outlets.
5. Motors overheat easily and often.
6. There is an excessive use of extension cords.

The number of uses to which electricity is put in the home is surprisingly large—and constantly growing. In order to ensure that your system can handle all your needs, use the wattage table to calculate the total wattage consumed in your home. If you are experiencing any of the problems mentioned above, you may be surprised with how much electricity you are actually using. This calculation will provide a helpful basis for planning future capacity should it be determined that rewiring is necessary.

Remember, however, that the list may not be absolutely complete, and also that the wattages shown may vary somewhat from manufacturer to manufacturer. They show, in general, the average electrical needs for each appliance listed.

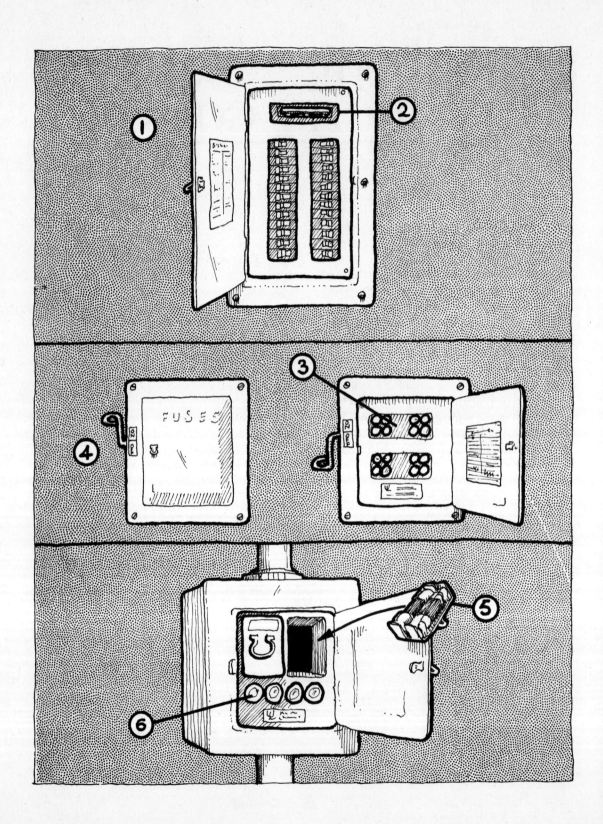

DISCONNECT!

We tend to take electricity for granted until it is suddenly no longer there. Then we realize to what a large extent we depend on it. The first step to having any control over the electricity in our domestic lives is to know where the service box is in the house. The service box, sometimes called the load center, is the place where the electricity that comes to the house can be switched on and off and distributed to the various circuits throughout the house. This is where fuses or circuit breakers are located. Since fuses preceded circuit breakers the service box is often referred to as the fuse box, even though it may contain no fuses, but only the more modern circuit breakers.

When anything goes wrong with the electrical system in the house, fuses or circuit breakers cause the power to be shut off, eliminating the possibilty of serious damage, such as a fire. Similarly, if *you* suspect that anything is wrong or potentially dangerous, or just want to work on the electrical system, you can disconnect the main electricity supply at the service box. The service box is thus the most important element in every house's electrical system, and it can be vitally important for you to know exactly where to find it.

The chances are that the service box will be found in a cupboard—cupboards under stairs are favorites—or in a closet. Sometimes it is located in the basement (but rarely in the attic); another frequently used location is in an attached garage. But no matter where it may be you should find it and make sure that it is accessible, especially in the dark. This means that if it is in a closet, it is not a good idea to store anything in front of it which would have to be removed before you could reach it. And it also means keeping a flashlight where it can be found easily (with your eyes shut), preferably next to the box itself.

Another important point to remember is that there may be more than one service box, especially in older houses which use the fuse-type box. An easy to check is to disconnect the first box you find and then see if anything electrical still works in the house. If the water heater is still working, for example, then you will know that it has its own service box.

How you turn off the current coming into the house depends on whether you have circuit breakers or fuses. If on opening the service center box you see rows of switches ①, with a larger switch at the top, usually marked "main" ②, you are looking at circuit breakers. In this case, all you have to do to disconnect the power is to flip the "main" switch.

Service boxes which contain fuses ③, on the other hand, often have a lever-type switch ④ which is outside the box, usually on the left-hand side. In this case, simply pull the lever down.

Alternatively, you may have to first open the box to disclose the cartridge-type "main" fuse ⑤. Cartridge fuses are located behind a pull-out plate which must be removed to shut off the power; and then you can safely remove the individual fuses ⑥.

You should never attempt any electrical repair without first turning off the main power and, if you are in any doubt, seek professional help. Once the power is safely off, you can effect the repairs outlined in the following pages with impunity. They are all simple, and purposely so. Not only can more complicated work be dangerous unless done by someone with experience, but in many places local building codes require electrical work to be done only by licensed electricians.

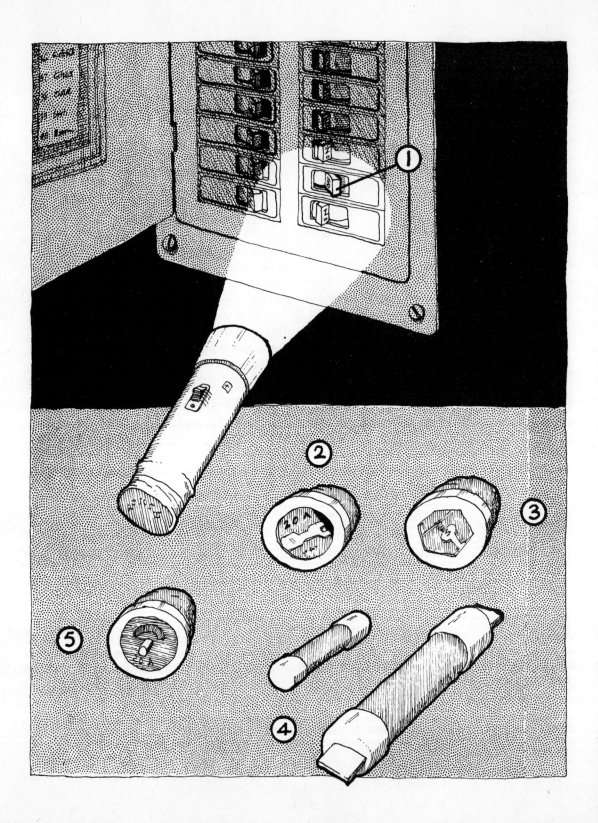

CIRCUIT BREAKERS AND FUSES

If an electrical circuit becomes overloaded for any reason, the power will be shut off to that circuit at the service box. This is accomplished either by a circuit breaker or a fuse. Before attempting to get the power back on (by resetting the circuit breaker or replacing the fuse), take some of the load off the circuit by unplugging or switching off appliances or lights.

Now proceed to the service box (see page 51). If it is equipped with circuit breakers, all you have to do is to look for the one that is in the "off" or "tripped" position ① and switch it back to the "on" position.

The various switches should be labeled so that you can identify which circuit is which. If the switches are not marked, you can identify them by a process of elimination. Turn everything on and note which switch controls which lights and appliances, etc. A word of warning: just because you find the breaker that controls the light in any particular room, that does not necessarily mean that neighboring outlets are "dead"—they may well be on a different circuit.

If your service box has fuses, they will probably be one of the various kinds shown in the illustration.

The plug fuse ② consists of a visible metal strip inside a glass screw-in unit. When the metal strip is broken or the glass has become blackened, the fuse is broken. It should be replaced by one of the same amperage.

The dual element fuse ③ has a spring-loaded metal strip that permits temporary overloading, such as occurs when an electric motor starts up.

A third type is the cartridge fuse ④. Big or small, the only way to know whether this type is blown or still working is to replace it with a known good fuse.

When something electrical stops working, the first job is to identify the blown fuse in the fuse box. Having first turned off other items on that circuit, shut off the main power, making sure that you are not standing on a wet floor and that you have a flashlight handy. Then unscrew or remove the fuse in question and replace it with a new fuse of the same amperage, and turn everything back on again. It is a good idea to maintain a supply of the fuses that your box contains so that you always have one handy.

The most common reason for a blown fuse is overloading—too much electricity being used at the same time. If a fuse blows immediately after having been replaced, but with fewer items operating, there may be damge somewhere in the circuit, such as a short in a loose plug or a frayed wire. At this point, unless you are a qualified electrician, call in professional help.

If you prefer the idea of circuit breakers but your house is equipped with plug fuses, you can replace them with "button breakers" ⑤ which look just like screw-in plug fuses with a button sticking out of the center. When this kind of breaker trips, the button pops out, and all you need to do is to push it back in to reset the fuse and reactivate the circuit.

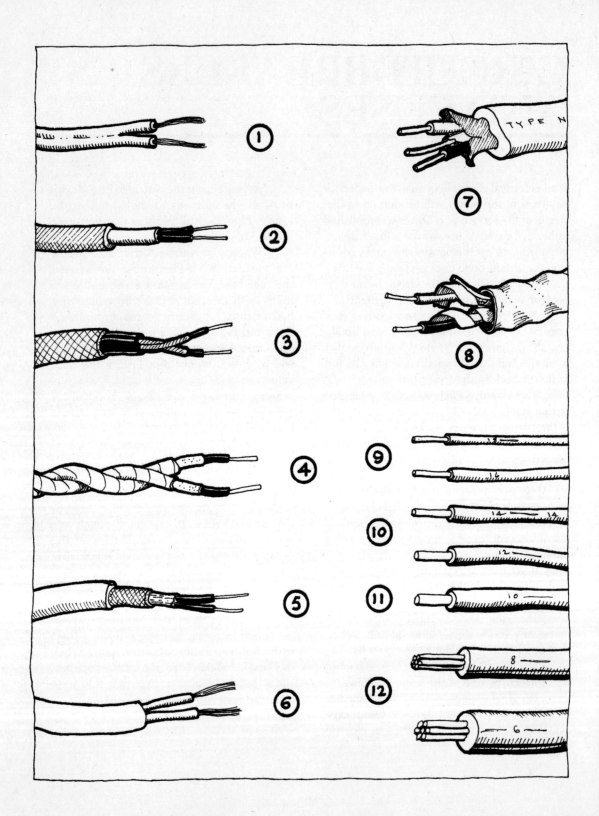

WIRE TYPES AND SIZES

Not all wire is the same, neither in size nor type, so it is very important to match the right wire to the job it has to do. The wire that connects various appliances to electric outlets is generally known as cord, and some of the various sorts are shown opposite.

① is stranded wire covered with rubber or plastic, commonly used as lamp cord. This cord is meant to carry no more than 1500 watts. Cords ② through ⑥ are used for heavy appliances, and all have two or more layers of insulation. ② is covered with rayon over an inner rubber insulation and is used in wet places, whereas ③, although rated for the same amount of current, is covered with fabric and is intended for use in dry locations. ④ is a braided cord with an inner asbestos lining and is used for heaters. ⑤ is fabric over rubber over jute over rubber, and ⑥ is simply sheathed with a heat-resistant thermoplastic.

House wiring is of two types. The commonest is the so-called Romex type ⑦, which is a plastic-sheathed cable containing two or three wires wrapped in paper. The older sort of armored cable ⑧ is known as BX. Whichever type of house wiring is used, the size may vary according to the job. The smaller the wire the larger the number by which it is known. Wire sizes 18 and 16 ⑨ are used mostly for flexible cords, but in the walls wire sizes 14 and 12 ⑩ are standard for most general circuits. Number 10 wire ⑪ is used for special circuits such as ranges and dishwashers. The two larger sizes shown, number 8 and number 6 wire ⑫, are used in circuits which have to carry 240 volts.

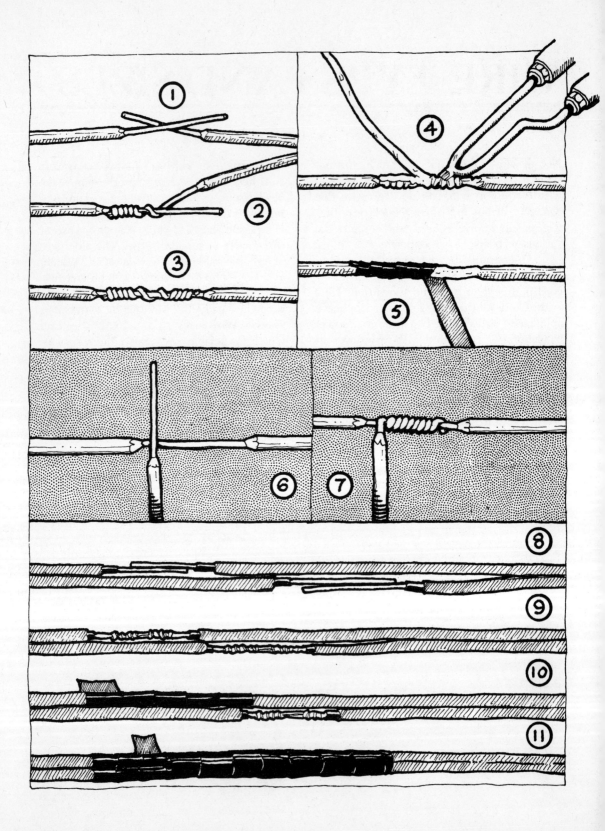

WIRE JOINTS AND SPLICES

The joining of two wires together is known as splicing and serves three purposes. First, it connects the two wires in such a way as to permit the electricity to flow from one to the other with the least amount of resistance. Second, it makes the connected wire as strong as a continuous piece of wire. Third, it insulates the wire as well as if it were a continuous piece, thus eliminating the possibility of a short circuit.

The steps in making a Western Union splice, which is the only appropriate splice when some pulling strain is to be expected, are shown in ① through ⑤. First, remove about 3 inches of insulation from the end of each wire ①. Second, after having made sure the ends are clean, and having crossed them over each other at their middle, wind the end of one of the wires tightly around the end of the other wire ②. Third, wind the end of the other wire around the end of the first wire ③. After having thoroughly heated the wire with a soldering iron, apply solder to the wire, which should be hot enough to cause the solder to melt onto it ④. If you just heat the solder and let it drip onto the wire it will not stick! Finally, wrap the soldered joint with insulating tape so that no wire or solder is left exposed ⑤.

When a wire must be joined to the middle of another wire the method used is known as a branch tap or a "T" splice. First, remove the insulation from the end of the joining wire and from the middle of the wire that is to be tapped into ⑥. Then cross the wires as shown, and twist the joining wire tightly around the exposed wire ⑦. Once again, the joint must be soldered and then wrapped with insulating tape.

To splice a two-wire cord requires that the joints be staggered so that the insulation on one side of the cord remains intact against the splice on the other side ⑧. When you are sure this has been done, join all four ends with Western Union splices as described above ⑨. The insulating should be done first individually ⑩, and then, when both splices have been covered, the whole should be wrapped with another layer of tape ⑪ for complete insulation.

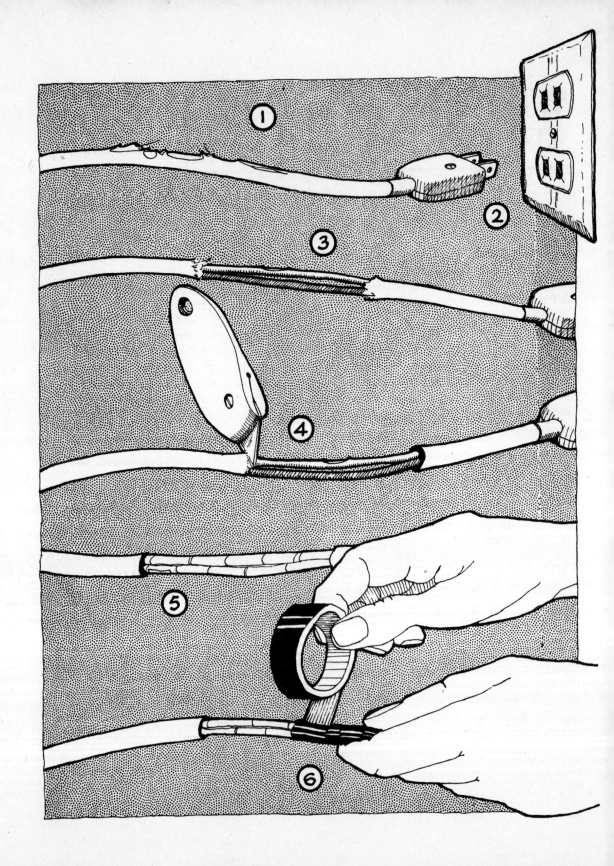

BARE WIRE!

Although the absolutely best thing to do when faced with damaged electrical wire is to discard it and replace it with new, there are some occasions when repair is acceptable—if only on a temporary basis. Nevertheless, it should be noted that you should *never* repair any damaged wire that forms part of the house's wiring—this definitely should be replaced.

The first thing to remember is that the smaller the wire, the greater is its resistance. Too much current along a wire with too high a resistance will cause the wire to heat up and possibly set something on fire. It is therefore of paramount importance that electrical wire of the right size for the intended load or job be used in every case. Never repair a damaged wire or electrical cord with wire that is thinner than the original.

The second thing to remember is that for wire to conduct electricity efficiently and safely, it must be properly insulated from other wires forming part of the cord and, indeed, from everything else around it. Torn, worn, otherwise damaged, or missing insulation around wiring can be very dangerous.

If you see bare wire caused by worn insulation in such places as lamp cords or other appliance cords ①, it should be replaced, but you can make it safe with the following temporary repair. Disconnect the electricity ② (by pulling the plug if it is a lamp cord, for example), and strip off the outer insulation about 1 inch or so in each direction from the damage ③.

At this point it should be noted that there are various types of cords suited for different purposes and different appliances, and they may all be constructed somewhat differently. Proceed with care until you are certain which kind you are dealing with.

Trim away any loose intermediate insulation ④, and wrap the bare wires, one at a time, with black electrical tape ⑤. This used to be made from cloth which tended to dry out and crumble away after a while, especially in warm locations, but nowadays it is more commonly made of plastic, which has a longer life and may be more easily stretched into shape. Wrap tightly, overlapping the tape half its width each turn, and extend the wrapping ½ inch on each side of the bare spot. Repeat the process for the neighboring wire (or wires), and then, holding both (or all) wires together, wrap them tightly, with another layer of tape, until the repaired section is as thick as the original cord ⑥. This repair will be safe, but should only be treated as temporary since it will not last as long as the rest of the cord.

When it is a matter of joining two wires together, the first thing that is necessary is to strip the ends of their insulation. This can be done with a knife, but it is much easier to use a special wire-stripper that will accommodate different thicknesses of wire. Never strip more than you need, and if you do use a knife, take care not to nick the wire—this weakens it. When the ends of the wire have been stripped, make sure that they are shiny bright—by scraping with a knife if necessary—to ensure a good electrical contact. Next, twist the two ends together in a clockwise direction. This is important because wire nuts, which are the most common means of joining two wires that have been twisted together, are threaded on the inside, and if you screw a wire nut onto two wires that have been twisted together in a counterclockwise fashion, you will simply be twisting them apart!

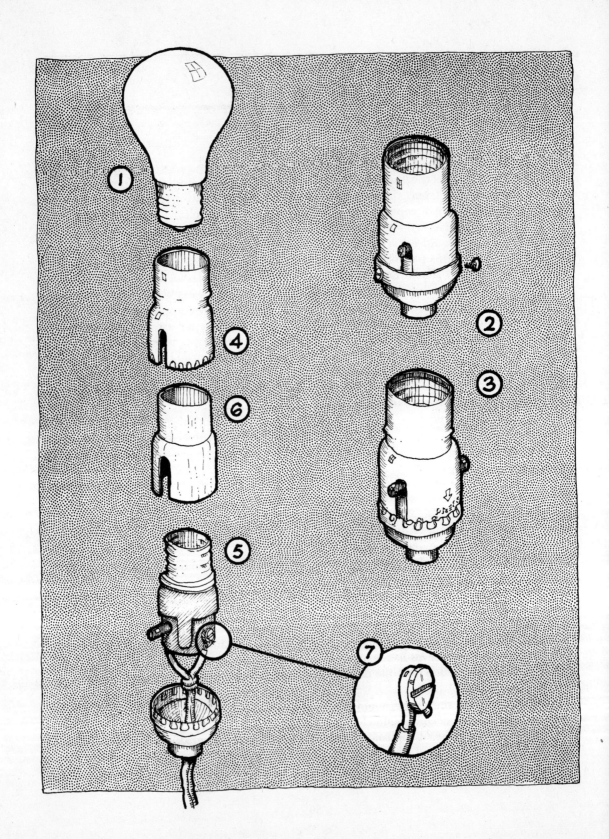

FLICKERING BULB

A flickering bulb can indicate several different problems, and even if the effect is not annoying enough to make you want to fix it right away, you should do so in any case since it could represent a potentially dangerous condition.

It might not be anything more serious than the bulb being too loose in its socket. This condition can occur frequently with bulbs that hang down from fixed wall sockets in places where there is a lot of vibration, such as from a heavily trafficked road or a nearby subway. The cure is simply to screw the bulb more firmly into its socket.

If, however, after tightening the bulb (gently), the flickering persists, turn on other lights on the same circuit. If they all flicker in unison while other lights in the house (on different circuits) burn steadily, this could indicate either a wiring problem in the service box or a problem outside the house on the utility pole. In either case call for professional help.

More likely than either of the above, however, is that the contact points in the bulb's socket have deteriorated. When this happens, replacement is the best remedy, and it is not difficult.

First, unplug the light, or if it has no visible wiring and cannot be unplugged, go to the service box and shut off the circuit to which the affected lamp is connected—or remove the appropriate fuse—and then check that the light is indeed off.

Second, remove the bulb ①; the socket is now ready for disassembly. The outer brass shell is made in two parts. Older sockets ②

were made with small screws which held the two parts together. Modern sockets ③, unfortunately, have dispensed with the screws and instead use an indented lower part which clips into the upper part. This system is nowhere near as secure, and care should be taken not to knock the two parts apart when the light is in use. Whichever sort you encounter, separate the two parts, by unscrewing the screw or by pressing the upper part in at the spot where "press" is etched into the metal. The top part, or shell ④, will now come away from the bottom part, or cap ⑤.

Inside you will discover a cardboard liner ⑥ which you should carefully put to one side. It constitutes the insulation between the wiring and the shell, without which a short circuit and the risk of shock is high. Now that the wires are exposed you can undo the terminal screws ⑦ holding them, and remove the socket from the fixture.

Before you attach a new socket, make sure that the wires are not brittle and cracked. If they are, cut off the damaged section and connect the socket to good, pliable wire. When you reassemble the new socket, do not forget the cardboard liner, for the reasons stated above.

Finally, screw in the bulb and turn the power back on; your problems should be over.

One last tip: if you have to remove a bulb which has shattered, make sure the light is unplugged or the circuit disconnected. Ball up a wad of paper and press it firmly into the broken bulb and turn.

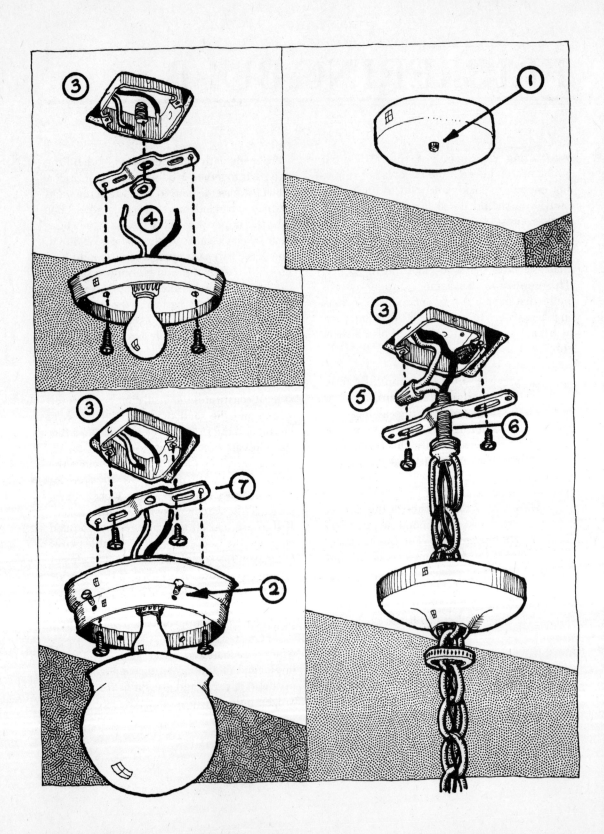

BROKEN CEILING FIXTURE

Once you understand the principles of the wiring involved, the hardest part of any ceiling fixture repair is often just figuring out how to remove the decorative cover.

For whatever reason it becomes necessary to work on a ceiling fixture, the method is the same. First, turn off the power to the circuit that the fixture is connected to. Just turning off a wall switch (if the light is so controlled) is not enough. Disconnect the circuit, and then double check the light. Next, remove the cover; as just mentioned, this can be quite baffling. There may be a single cap nut in the center ①, several screws or nuts around the edge ②, or the cover itself may lift or twist off. But somehow you must remove the shade or cover attached to the electrical box ③ which actually houses the wiring to which the wires in the fixture are attached.

To completely disconnect the fixture from the ceiling, so that you can work on it at ground level, or so that it can be replaced, you must disconnect the wiring. Recent work will consist of black wires and white wires ④. Bearing in mind that black connects to black and white connects to white, you should have no difficulty in reconnecting everything correctly when the time comes. If the fixture is old, it might not be so readily apparent which wire connects to which when you come to the reassembly. If this is the case, make a note now, before you actually disconnect anything, of what goes where.

The wires will either be spliced together or held together with wire nuts ⑤. Wire nuts are easy to remove. Remember to twist them off counterclockwise—they are threaded inside in order to grip the wire better. If the wires are spliced together, unwrap any insulating tape covering the splice and snip them apart, leaving as much wire on the fixture as you can.

Now the fixture can either be worked upon or be replaced by another fixture.

Installing a ceiling fixture requires that the electric box through which the wires emerge in the ceiling ③ be fitted with the appropriate straps or studs for holding the fixture. Sometimes, a fixture that is designed to hang from a central threaded stud ⑥ requires a different size stud than exists in the box. This can be accommodated by obtaining a reducing nut and nipple from the hardware store. If the fixture is held by screws at its edge rather than from a central stud, you need the slotted strap ⑦ that screws to the electric box and to which, in turn, the fixture itself is mounted.

Once you have got the right hardware it is simply a matter of connecting the right wires together again and then reassembling the fixture. Just remember that when connecting the wires there should be no bare wire left showing, and all wire nuts should be screwed on securely—clockwise. Also, the wire in new fixtures may need to be trimmed a little. While it is necessary to have enough slack in the wire so that the fixture can be pulled apart, the box should not be stuffed with excess wire.

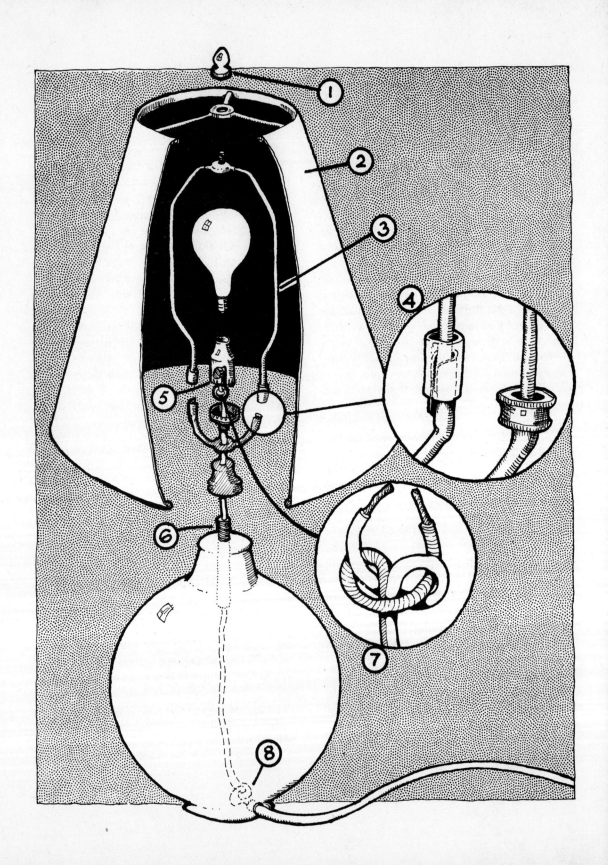

TABLE LAMP REPAIR

Table lamps can be relatively fragile, and can suffer all kinds of damage. Unless the actual lamp is shattered beyond repair, all kinds of things can be put right to make a favorite lamp work, if you understand basic lamp anatomy.

The shade is commonly attached to a harp which is connected to the socket that holds the bulb. The socket is generally connected to the lamp by a threaded rod which is held in the lamp either by cork or nuts at the neck of the lamp (if it is the common vase-shape), or by a plate at the base of the lamp. The wiring normally passes through this rod.

The disassembly process for the repair or replacement of any given part is as follows: unscrew the cap nut ① that holds the shade ② to the harp ③, and remove the shade. Replace the cap nut on the harp for safe keeping.

Remove the harp by pressing its bottom end inwards and slipping up the tube connectors ④ that hold it in place. Sometimes there are little finger nuts instead of these sliding connectors, but in either case the harp simply pulls free.

The next step is to remove the socket ⑤. This is threaded onto a rod ⑥ through which the wiring passes, and it may be necessary to free the bottom of the wiring where it enters the lamp before you can unscrew the socket. If you don't free the wire, unscrewing the socket will twist the wire, possibly to the point of collapse. To gain access to the wiring you may have to remove the base of the lamp. If this is just felt, slice it off carefully with a very sharp knife. Alternatively, the socket rod may extend all the way to the base and be secured there by a nut, which when undone will allow access to the interior of the lamp and removal of the socket at the same time.

Removal of the threaded rod is rarely necessary. Usually everything else will screw off, leaving it still in place, but if you must remove the rod, look for the nut which holds it to the lamp where it passes through the neck, underneath the socket.

Disassembly of the actual socket is the same as described on page 61, but something else should be noted here. The end of the wire should have the so-called underwriters' knot tied in it ⑦ before its connection to the terminals of the socket. This knot is a precaution against the wires pulling loose through the bottom of the socket. If you are replacing the wire, do not forget to replace this knot. As a further precaution tie another (regular) knot where the wire passes through the base of the lamp ⑧, in order to prevent it from pulling through here, too.

Start reassembling the lamp by slipping the harp base onto the threaded rod, followed by the cap (bottom part) of the socket—which often has a small screw in its neck to hold it firmly to the rod. Then push the wire up through the rod, tie the underwriters' knot in the end and connect it to the terminals of the socket. Install the socket as outlined on page 61.

All that remains is to secure the base of the lamp and screw the shade back on.

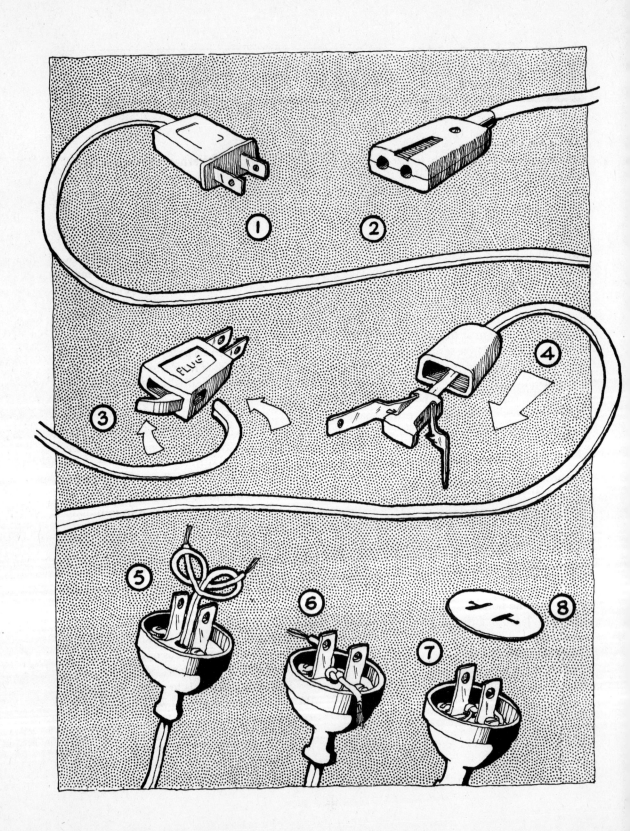

REPLACEMENT PLUG

Every cord that connects any kind of appliance, large or small, to the house's circuitry does so with a plug whose prongs plug into wall outlets. This kind of plug is known as a male plug ①. There are also female plugs ②; these are used on various appliances such as electric frying pans and waffle makers, and connect the cord to the appliance.

Most plug replacements are made necessary by worn or cracked wiring—it's not the plug that has worn out but the rewiring that makes it necessary to fit a plug to a new cord. Sometimes, however, plugs do need replacing as a result of a cracked shell or loose prongs. Any plug that sparks when inserted into or removed from an outlet needs attention and possibly replacement (usually the terminals are loose). Some plugs cannot be disassembled; they are molded together and have no visible screws or other means of inserting or removing the wires. These plugs should be replaced if the appliance they serve begins to work erratically, or if the plug itself becomes warm to the touch when in use.

There are many varieties of plug. When replacing one, the safest thing to do, if you are not sure which type is best, is to use the same sort as the original. The simplest type is the so-called "self-connecting" plug. The wire is simply pushed into the plug or its cap, and snapping a clamp shut ③, or putting the cap back on the plug ④, causes little interior teeth to bite into the wire—and the connection is made. While these plugs remove the need to strip wire and mess about with screws and tiny terminals, they are basically light-duty plugs and should only be used for small appliances that are infrequently plugged in and out, such as radios and lamps. In fact, most are only big enough to accept lamp cord.

Other male plugs, while manufactured in a variety of shapes and sizes, all operate on the same principle, whether they have two or three prongs. (Some of these are molded, too, and cannot be repaired, only replaced.) The simplest thing to do is to cut the cord as close to the plug as you can, in order to preserve as much of the cord's length as possible. The outer insulation of the cord should be stripped back about 2 or 3 inches to reveal the wires still covered by the inner insulation. If the cord is lamp cord, also known as zip cord, it will have no outer insulation. Separate the two strands by cutting between them carefully, so as not to damage the insulation. The separation should also be about 2 or 3 inches long.

Now thread the cord through the base of the plug, make an underwriters' knot in the end of the wire ⑤, and pull it back snugly against the base of the plug ⑥. This provides a means of protecting the terminals from being strained should the plug be yanked from the outlet by the cord. (This is not a recommended practice, but is something to which nearly every cord is invariably subjected.)

Strip the very ends of the wire clean, and, if it is stranded wire, twist the ends clockwise to keep the strands together. A drop of solder is sometimes recommended at this point but it usually makes the wire too bulky to fit around the terminal. Just be sure that you wind the wire around the terminal in a clockwise fashion ⑦—so that when the screw is turned in it takes the wire with it instead of pushing it out. Also, make sure that the wire touches nothing except the terminal—or electrical shorts will result.

Finally, replace any insulating cap ⑧. This is usually a cardboard disc, but is sometimes a screw-on piece of plastic.

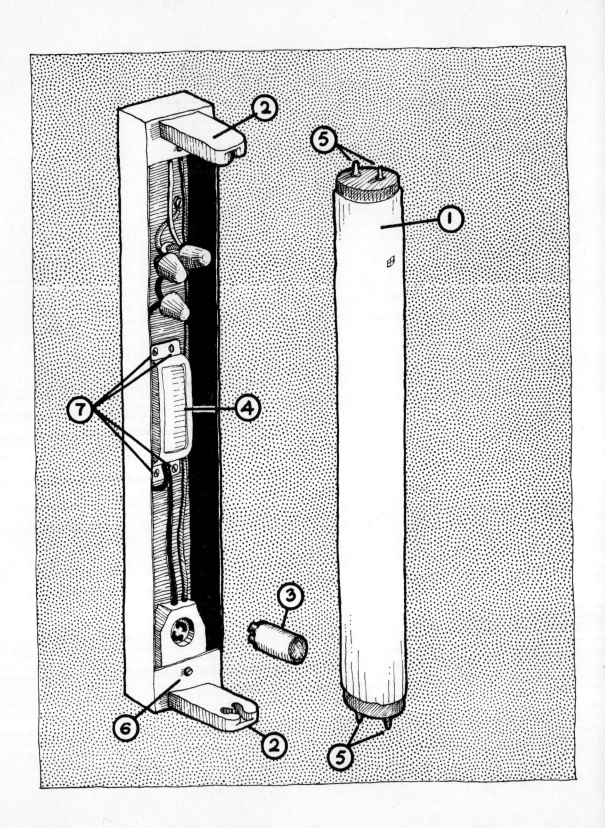

FLUORESCENT TROUBLES

The inside of a fluorescent lamp or tube is coated with phosphor that glows as a result of energy transmitted to it by heated mercury vapor inside the tube. The mercury vapor is heated by special filaments at the end of the tube. Although this sounds a little more complicated than the simple glowing of a filament in an incandescent light bulb, the fluorescent lamp is far more efficient, and indeed there are really only four parts that can give any trouble. These are the tube itself ① (which normally lasts much longer than an incandescent light bulb), the sockets ② which hold the tube—one at each end, the starter ③, and the ballast ④.

The tube normally becomes dark at the ends, but if it begins to turn very dark or even black, then this is a warning that it will soon wear out completely.

If the tube flickers a lot, then the first thing to check is whether or not it is seated properly in the sockets. The pins ⑤ in the tube should first be aligned with the slots on the socket, the tube pushed into place, and then twisted a quarter turn. It could also be that the contacts require a light sanding.

Furthermore, the sockets themselves, which are usually secured by small mounting screws ⑥, may be loose and require tightening. If the actual sockets become damaged it is usually possible to remove them and obtain replacements—but take the old ones along to make sure you get exactly the right sort.

If the tube still flickers a lot, especially after starting, then the trouble is probably in the starter. The starter ③ can usually be found by removing the tube. It is a small cylindrical device which is removed by being pressed down and turned. The starter heats the filaments until the lamp lights, then it automatically cuts off and the lamp continues to glow without it. The only way to test a starter is by replacing it with a known good one—such as a new one. Be sure to get one with the same capacity. Another reason to replace a starter that causes the tube to flicker a lot before properly lighting is that a defective starter shortens the tube life quite considerably.

If the starter is good, then the tube may be wearing out, but if both tube and starter are good then the problem may be that it is too cold! Most fluorescent lamps are designed to operate at 50 degrees Fahrenheit or more. If conditions are commonly colder (such as in an unheated basement or garage), get a special low-temperature tube and a thermal starter.

Also, be aware that new tubes commonly flicker a bit more than usual when first turned on, but that this tendency diminishes as the tube is used for a while.

If the whole assembly hums loudly, it is probably the fault of the ballast ④. This device is like a transformer, regulating the amount of current fed to the lamp, and it sometimes vibrates loose. Try tightening the mounting screws ⑦. If it still hums it is possible to replace it with low-noise ballast—but take the original along to make sure you get the right kind.

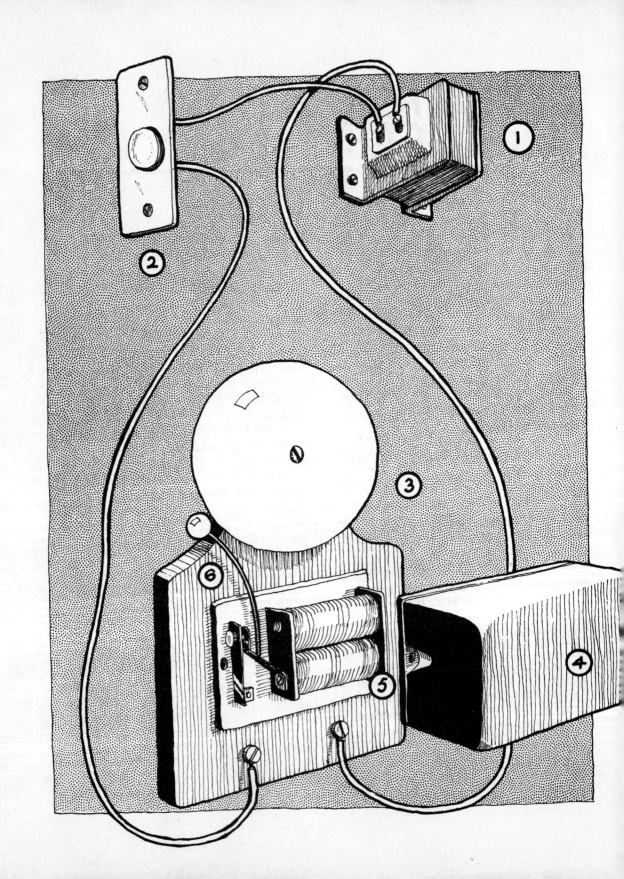

BROKEN DOORBELL

When your doorbell or chimes won't work at all, won't stop working, or only works intermittently no matter how hard you press the push button, do not despair—the repair is usually quite simple.

It doesn't take much current to operate a bell or chimes. A little device called a transformer ① is used between the house wiring and the actual unit to reduce the voltage from 120 volts to somewhere between 12 and 24 volts—depending on how many buzzers, bells, or push buttons are involved. Despite this low voltage it is still a good idea to turn off the electricity before working on any of the parts—you could still get a painful, if not lethal, shock.

Since the button ② at the door is usually exposed to the elements, check this part first if nothing happens when it is pressed. Take it apart carefully, and make sure that the contacts are shiny clean, and that all the wires are connected—but only to the right terminals, and not to each other as a result of having become frayed or broken. Make sure that the button is free to move in and out when pressed and released and is not clogged with debris. A quick check can be made by unscrewing the two wires that come to the push button and, holding them by their insulated part, touching the exposed wires together. When the current is on this should produce results. If not, move on to the next step.

The next step involves an inspection of the sound unit ③. Bells and chimes which are located in kitchens are particularly susceptible to grease and dirt clogging up the works, but even if the unit is located in a hallway, an inspection will often turn up a surprising amount of dirt.

It may be that the wiring and the contacts are dirty, and need to be cleaned and even scraped shiny bright, or it may be that dirt has impeded the movement of the moving parts. Remove the cover ④, and you will see the wires that run to the button and the transformer, and a copper-wound device known as the electromagnet ⑤. The electromagnet either moves small pins backwards and forwards to strike the chimes, or moves a spring armature ⑥ with a hammer on the end that hits a bell or bells. All of these parts should be cleaned free of dust and lint, and the chimes or bells inspected to see that they are mounted securely and not jammed—which could prevent their sounding when struck.

If the sounding unit appears to be in good order then you should now check the wiring. Since the voltage used is low, the wire is generally quite thin and consequently subject to becoming brittle and breaking. If the wire disappears into the wall, the best course is to rewire the whole length.

Finally, there is always the chance that the transformer has broken. This is a small, cheap unit ① usually found close to either the button or the service box. A quick test is to hold a piece of wire across the terminals on the low-voltage side of the transformer—the side to which the thin wires are connected. If there is power, a small spark will occur and you will know that the problem is in the wiring from that point on. No spark means a new transformer may be required.

If the bell should go on and stay on, there is a short in the wiring. Simply cut one of the wires to stop the ringing, and then trace the whole circuit for worn or frayed spots.

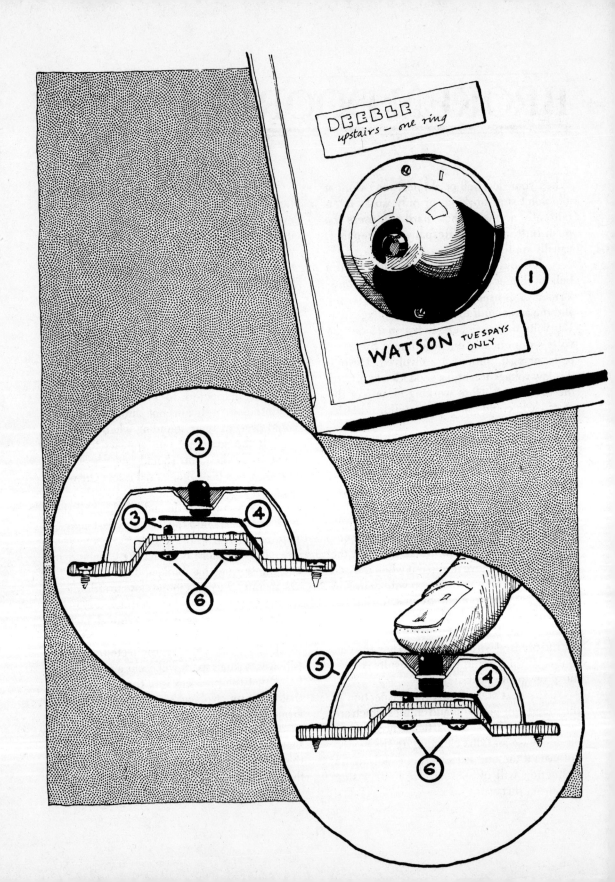

BUZZER BREAKDOWN

The push button ① that operates the doorbell or buzzer is simply a switch. Electricity cannot flow through a circuit if that circuit is interrupted, and this is the function of a switch—to interrupt and reconnect a circuit.

A buzzer "switch" keeps the circuit interrupted until someone presses the button. Pushing the button ② brings the two contact points ③ together, completes the circuit, and causes electricity to flow through the circuit causing the bell or buzzer to sound.

The button is held in place and attached by a spring ④, so that when the pressure is released it automatically springs back, breaking the circuit once again and causing the bell or buzzer to stop sounding.

If it fails to work, and you know there is current going to the buzzer, remove the cap ⑤ and inspect the button to make sure that it can move freely and yet is still held in place by the spring. Inspect the contact points to see that they are clean and shiny. Once they become corroded it is difficult for electricity to flow between them, even though they touch. If this is the case, clean them by rubbing them with some fine sandpaper until they shine again.

Finally, inspect the terminals ⑥ to which the wires are attached to see that everything is still firmly connected and that nothing is touching anything that it shouldn't. These points are also subject to corrosion and must be kept similarly clean.

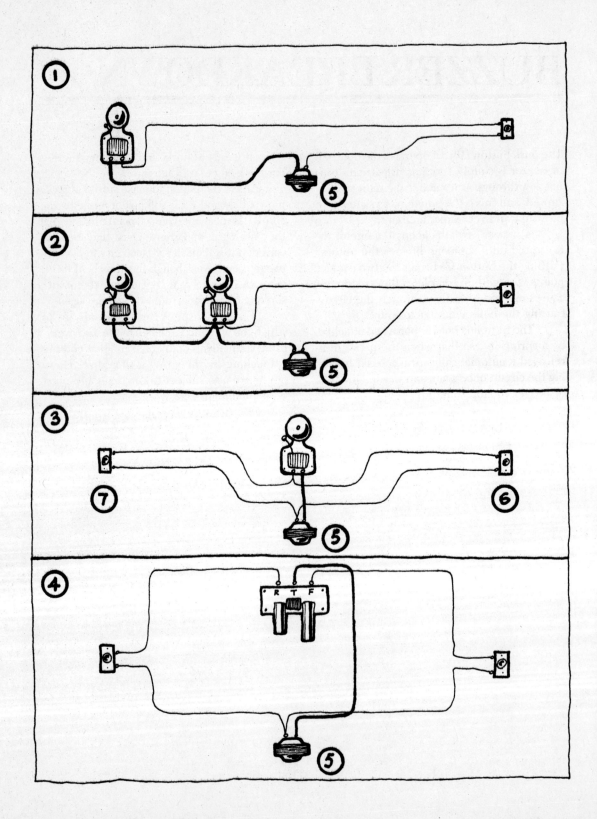

BELL AND CHIME CIRCUITS

A basic knowledge of how the doorbell or chime circuit works will enable you to fix, alter, or augment whatever system you may have at present, or to install one if you have none.

The simplest form is the circuit shown in ①, whereby one door button works one bell. (For clarity's sake only, the wire from the transformer to the bell or chimes is shown as a heavy black line—in reality this wire need be no different from any of the other wires.)

If you live in a large house and a single bell located in one part of the house would not be heard somewhere else, then the two-bell system ② might be used to good advantage. No matter where the second bell is located, the same terminal should be used for the transformer wire as is used on the first bell, and the other terminal used for the extension of the doorbell button wire.

If one bell can be heard all over the house, but you would like a button at the front door ⑥ and a second button at the back door ⑦, as shown in ③, then simply wire the back door button to the same terminals used by the front door button—that is, leave the transformer alone.

A fourth variation ④ is even more sophisticated. This system provides for two buttons, one at the front door and one at the back door. By using chimes that have three terminals instead of the two that most bells have, you can tell whether it is the front door button or the back door button that has been pressed.

When the front door button (which is wired to the terminal on the chimes marked "F") is pressed, the front door striker is moved to hit the short chime. When the button is released the striker springs back and hits the long chime, producing a nice "ding-dong!" But when the back door button (which is wired to the terminal on the chimes marked "R"—for rear door) is pressed, although the back door striker hits the short chime, on release it does not hit the long chime because it is blocked in some way, and thus only a "ding" is produced! Only chimes with two strikers can do this, but you do not have to worry about counting the strikers because if the chimes have three terminals, you can take it for granted that there are two strikers inside.

One last tip. In order to make life a little easier when wiring up the more complicated systems, use the special color-coded three-stranded bell wire that is available at most hardware stores. This will help you make sure that you have the same wire connected to the proper terminals.

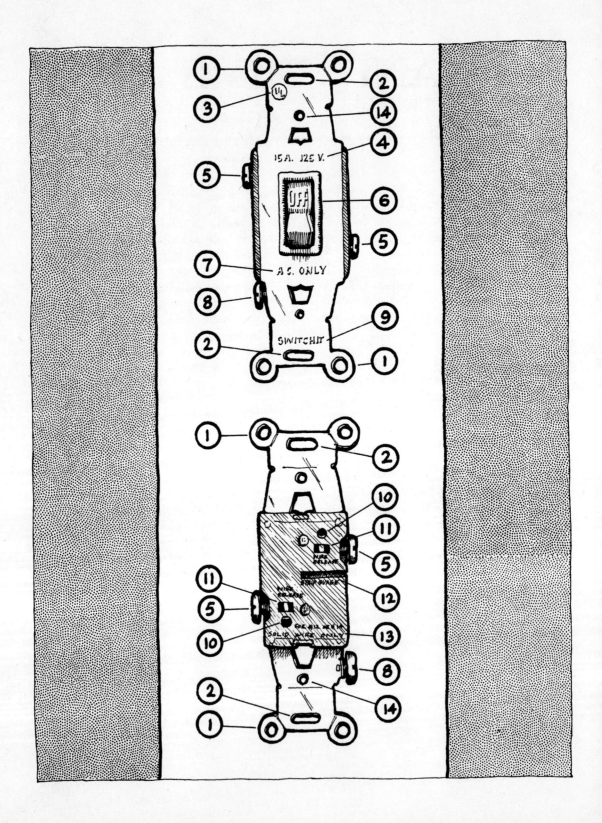

SWITCH INFORMATION

The common light switch that pokes out through its face plate, and whose removal and installation is described on page 79, contains a wealth of information about itself if you know where to look. The illustration shows the front and back view of a typical switch, and lists the things you ought to know about it:

① These little ears are used for mounting the switch to certain kinds of outlet boxes. If they are not used and are in the way, they may be broken off by being bent backwards and forwards a few times.

② This slot holds the screw that most commonly holds the switch to the outlet box in which it is mounted. It is slotted in order to allow for a certain amount of sideways adjustment in the event that the outlet box is not mounted perfectly straight in the wall.

③ This little sign signifies that the switch has been approved by the testing authority known as the Underwriters' Laboratory, is safe, and conforms to electrical code.

④ The amperage and voltage rating is stamped into each switch. In this case the switch is rated for 15 amps and 120 volts—as are most switches of this type.

⑤ One of the screw terminals to which the wiring may be attached. There may be two, three, or four of these screws depending on the purpose of the switch (described in more detail on page 79). They may be either silver or brass-colored.

⑥ The only part of the switch normally visible—the toggle. Depending on whether this is a two-way or a three- or four-way switch it may or may not be marked "on" and "off."

⑦ This indicates the type of current that the switch is designed for, in this case alternating current (AC).

⑧ This little screw is usually colored green and is the terminal to which the ground wire must be attached. Older switches did not always have a ground screw and should be changed to the newer type which offers more protection.

⑨ Somewhere on any switch you will probably find the manufacturer's trademark or name.

⑩ As well as being able to connect the wiring to the terminal screws, some switches provide push-in terminals which may be used instead of the screws.

⑪ Once the wire is in the push-in terminal, the only way to get it out is by inserting a small screwdriver into this slot, often marked "wire release," and pushing hard while at the same time pulling the wire hard.

⑫ The strip gauge provides an easy way to know how much insulation to strip off the end of a wire you wish to insert into the push-in terminal.

⑬ There are various types and sizes of wire. Not all of them are suitable for use in any given switch, so there is usually an indication of the preferred type stamped on the switch—in this case number 12 or number 14 solid wire (see page 55 for wire types and sizes).

⑭ This little hole, which is threaded, receives the screw that holds the face plate to the switch.

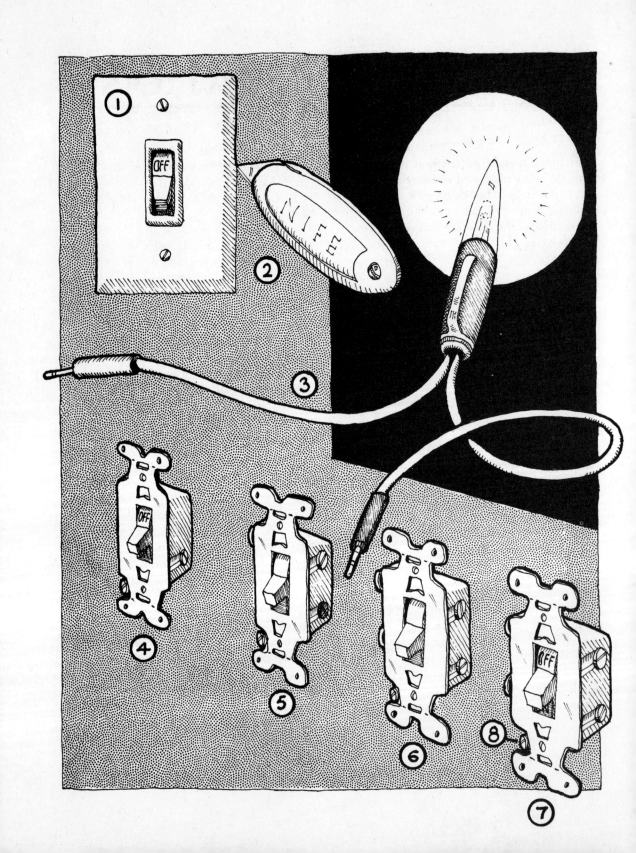

FAULTY LIGHT SWITCH

Switch actions wear out, contacts oxidize, fuses blow whenever switches are operated—this all means it is time to replace the switch.

Do nothing until you are sure the power to the switch you intend to work on is off. If you're not sure about which circuit a particular switch is on, turn off the main breaker switch.

Unscrew and remove the face plate ①. If this has been painted over you will cause less paint to chip away from the wall when you remove the plate by first scoring around the plate with a sharp razor knife ②. With the plate removed, pull the switch out a little way. Double check that the power is off with the help of a voltage tester ③. This is an inexpensive tool readily available at most hardware stores. Put one of its wires against the metal of the switch box—which you should now be able to see in the wall—and the other wire against each of the terminal screws on the switch in turn. If the voltage tester lights up or glows, there is still power coming to the switch!

When you are sure that the power is really off, remove the switch from the box by gently pulling it as far forward as it will go. At this point carefully examine the switch to determine what sort of replacement you should install.

The single-pole switch ④ is the most common. This has only two terminals, both usually brass-colored. It is used for a simple on-off control of a light or an outlet.

A three-way switch ⑤ is used as one of a pair of such switches to control a light or outlet from two different places. The toggle will not have "on" or "off" marked on it since these positions change as one or other of the pair of switches is used. There are three terminals on a three-way switch, and one of them should be a darker color than the other two.

A four-way switch ⑥ is used in combination with other four-way switches to control a light or outlet from three or more places. This switch also has no "on" or "off" markings. Inside, it has four similarly colored terminals.

A double-pole switch ⑦ does the same job as a single-pole switch and so has "on" and "off" marked on the toggle, but it has four terminals and is used for 240 volt appliances only.

Although you have no choice about the former types—you *must* use a similar replacement and connect the wires in exactly the same places as on the original—you do have a choice of styles. There are mercury switches, push-button switches, and even delayed-action switches. Inside, however, they will all be the same as the original.

Older switches had no ground screw ⑧ but new switches do. When installing a new switch in a box which previously housed an old-type switch, you must add an extra length of ground wire connecting the ground screw on the switch to the ground wire of the wiring. This ground wire must also be connected to a screw on the metal box holding the switch.

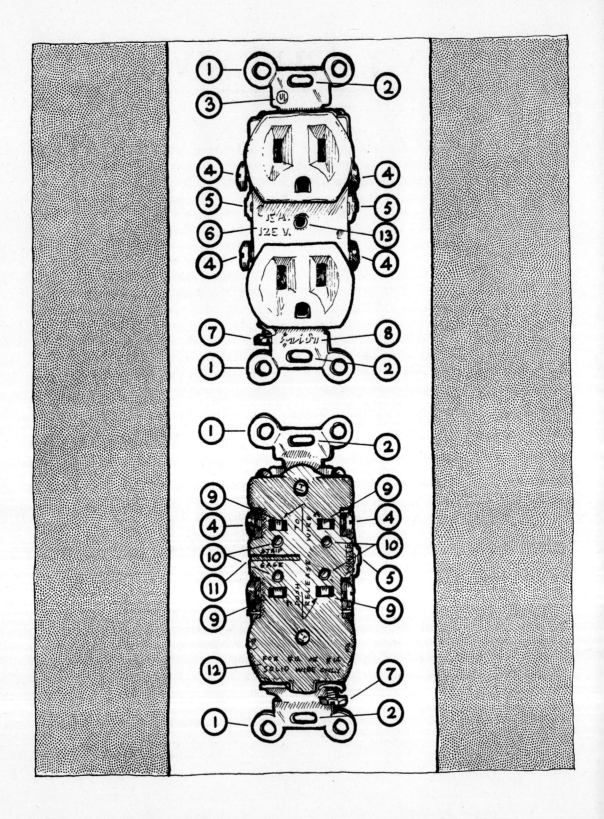

OUTLET INFORMATION

Unlike switches, most outlets apart from combination-switch outlets, are all practically the same. But like switches, outlets contain a lot of information describing their proper use and application which is useful to know. The front and back views of an outlet, sometimes called a duplex receptacle, illustrate this:

① These little ears are used for mounting the outlet to certain kinds of outlet boxes. If they are not being used and are in the way they may be broken off by being bent backwards and forwards a few times.

② This slot holds the screw that most commonly holds the outlet to the outlet box in which it is mounted. It is slotted in order to allow for a certain amount of sideways adjustment in the event that the outlet box is not mounted perfectly straight in the wall.

③ This little sign signifies that the outlet has been approved by the testing authority known as the Underwriters' Laboratory, is safe, and conforms to electrical code.

④ One of the terminal screws to which the wiring may be attached. On one side of the outlet these screws are brass-colored. The black wires are attached to these. The screws on the other side are silver-colored. The white wires are attached to these. To make the matter even clearer, "white" is stamped into the back of the outlet next to the silver-colored terminals.

⑤ For some wiring purposes it is necessary to break the contact between the upper part of the outlet and the lower part. This is done by breaking off these brass tabs which form the electrical contact.

⑥ The amperage and voltage rating is stamped into each outlet. In this case the outlet is rated for 15 amps and 120 volts.

⑦ This little screw is usually colored green and is the terminal to which the ground wire must be attached. Older outlets did not always have a ground screw and should be changed to the newer type which affords more protection.

⑧ Somewhere on most outlets you may find the manufacturer's name or trademark.

⑨ As well as being able to connect the wiring to the terminal screws, some outlets provide push-in terminals which may be used instead of the screw terminals.

⑩ Once the wire is in the push-in terminal it cannot be removed without first pressing a small screwdriver into this hole, which is marked "push here to release" on the back of this outlet.

⑪ The strip gauge provides an accurate measurement of the amount of insulation which should be removed from the end of a wire that you wish to insert in a push-in terminal.

⑫ This indicates the correct wire type and size to be used.

⑬ This is the little threaded hole which receives the screw that holds the face plate to the outlet.

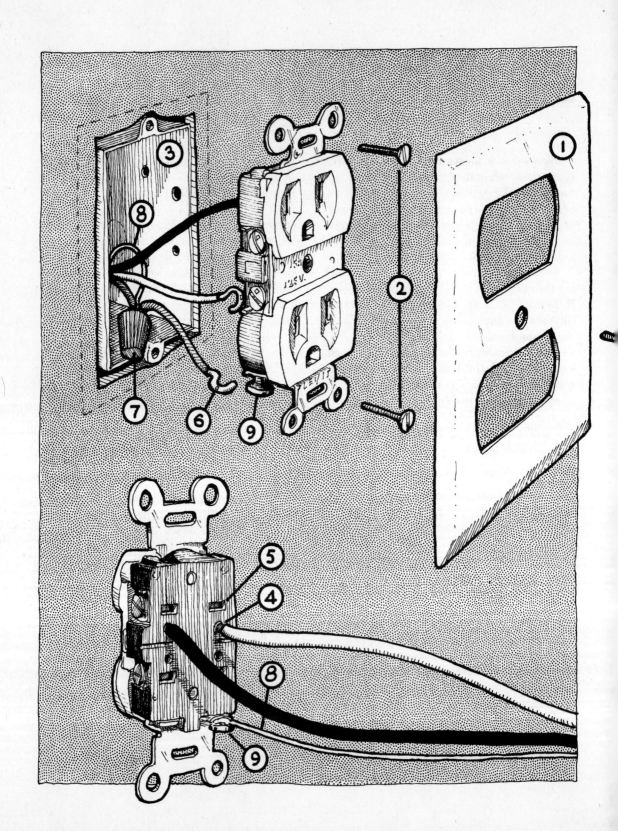

DEFECTIVE OUTLET

Outlets need to be replaced for various reasons. They may no longer hold a plug securely; they may cause radios which are plugged into them to crackle and hiss; or they may simply have to give way to a more specialized outlet, such as one with a snap cover to protect exploring children from sudden shocks.

Before you even remove the face plate ①, make absolutely certain that the power is off, even if this means pulling the main switch and shutting down everything in the whole house.

Score around the face plate, if it has been painted over, to avoid removing too much paint from the wall when you pull off the plate (see ① page 79).

Loosen the screws ② at the top and bottom of the outlet that hold it to the box ③, which may be metal or plastic, and gently pull the outlet forward until you can see the wires that are attached to the outlet. The number of wires you see will depend in part on where the outlet is in the circuit. For example, if it is the last outlet on the circuit you may see only two wires (and perhaps a ground wire), but elsewhere in the circuit there may be as many as five wires connected to the back of the outlet.

There are two methods of connecting the wires. The first way involves terminal screws—the removal of wires from these is obvious. The second uses push-in terminals

④ from which the wire is released by inserting a screwdriver into a slot ⑤ in the back of the outlet next to the little hole into which the wire disappears. In fact, on many outlets the instruction "push wire release" is stamped into the plastic. In either case, remove the wires and be certain to reconnect them to exactly the same places in the new outlet. One sure way of doing this is to remove only one wire at a time and immediately connect it to the new outlet.

If you are using terminal screws, remember to twist the end of the wire into a clockwise loop ⑥ before connecting it around the screw. This way, the tightening of the screw will pull the wire closer to the screw instead of pushing it away from it. A pair of needle-nose pliers is the best tool for making the necessary loop. Similarly, remember to twist the wires that are to be held with a wire nut ⑦ together in a clockwise fashion, since these are threaded inside and are screwed on clockwise. No bare wire, except for the ground wire ⑧, should be showing after everything has been connected, prior to the outlet being pushed back into its box.

Of the three wires that form part of the house wiring, one is white, one is black, and one is bare. The bare wire is the ground wire, which should be connected to any other bare wire that leaves the box, a screw on the box itself, and to the green screw ⑨ which is found on all new outlets.

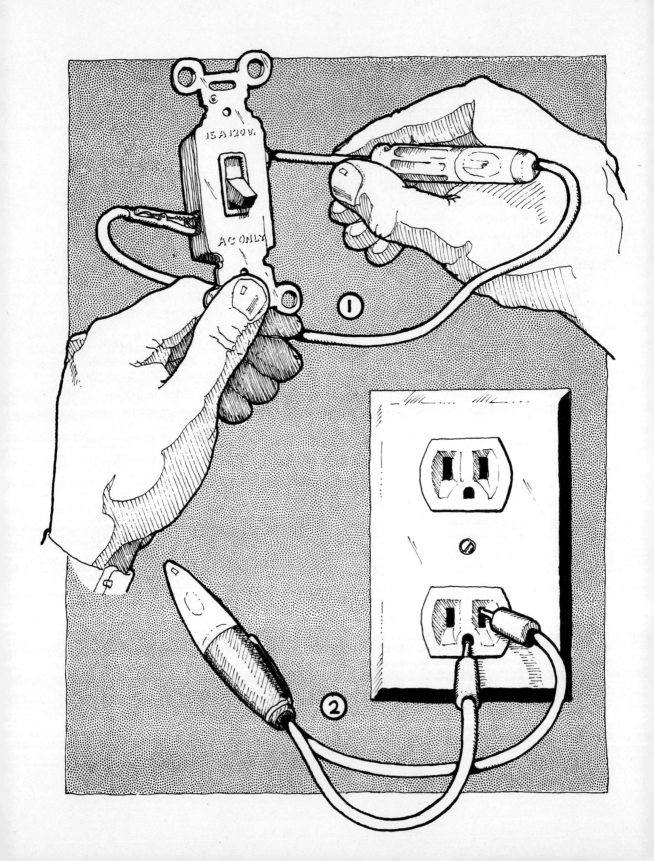

TESTERS

Professional electricians may have all kinds of equipment—including a variety of testing instruments that measure and check current, resistance, volts, ohms, etc. However, there are two simple testers that the average householder might profitably use. These will be of value when making some of the simple repairs outlined in the previous pages, while costing very little and requiring little expertise to use, and represent a considerable investment in your efficiency.

The continuity tester ① is a device that lights up if something that is being tested is in working order. If you suspect a switch, for example, of not working properly, you may test it with the continuity tester.

First, to be absolutely safe, disconnect the switch from the wiring, following the precautions outlined on page 79, and then attach the alligator clip of the tester to one of the terminals on the switch. If everything is in order, when you touch the probe of the tester to the other terminal, a light will glow in the tester.

Since the continuity tester is self-powered, you must of course make sure that its battery is in good order before you can expect it to work. When it does it can be inval-uable in checking out something that cannot be seen by the eye alone.

It can also be used to check continuity in anything else through which, when properly connected, electricity is supposed to flow.

The voltage tester ② does not need a battery, since it glows when electric current is present. Whenever you have occasion to make sure that the power is off at some point, use the voltage tester to check that this is indeed so. If, for example, you are working on an electric outlet and *think* you have turned off the power correctly at the service box, double check with the voltage tester. If it glows when used, the power is not yet off!

To check an outlet simply insert one lead of the tester into the hot-wire slot and touch the other to the ground-prong hole, or, if the outlet is the two-hole type, touch the other lead to the little screw that holds the face plate on (see the illustration on page 83).

Similarly, you can use it to connect any two wires that run to an appliance. If the power to that appliance is off (which is not the same thing as the appliance itself being switched off!), the tester will remain dead, but if it glows—beware, the power is still on.

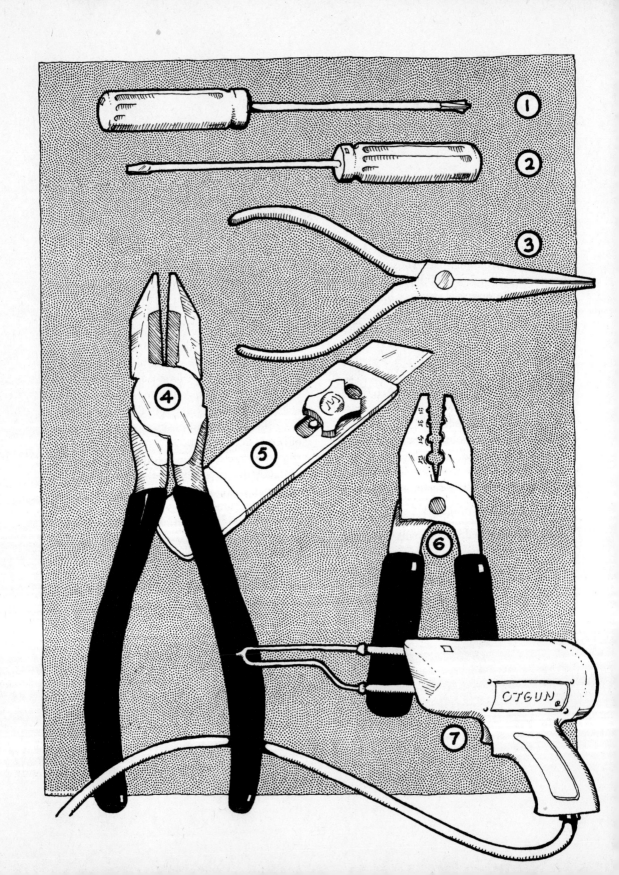

TOOLS

Apart from the testers described on the previous pages, the electrical jobs you may undertake with the help of this book call for very few tools.

A couple of screwdrivers, one with a Phillips point ① and one with a straight blade ② are indispensable, and are to be found in almost every house. For electrical work long and narrow ones are most useful, although every now and then a larger straight screwdriver may come in very handy.

Needle-nose pliers ③ are not only good for holding small things in tight corners where your fingers can't reach, but they are also the best tool for bending wire into loops when attaching it to screw terminals (see ⑦ page 61).

A stout pair of electrician's pliers with insulated handles will hold things, twist things, and even cut things (such as wire). Too often, however, they are allowed to get wet and dirty, and consequently can become very hard to open and close. By keeping them clean, and putting a drop of oil on the joint once in a while, you will save yourself much aggravation.

There are many different designs of razor knives ⑤ available. Choose whichever one pleases you, but see that it has a retract-able blade, and, if possible, replacement blades. Sometimes blades come stored in the handle, and sometimes the old point may be broken off when it becomes dull to reveal a new edge.

Wire strippers ⑥ are a specialized tool used solely for electrical work and whose usefulness cannot be emphasized too much. The various size holes in the jaw are for gripping different size wires (see the wire chart on page 54) and are frequently marked with the size wire for which each hole is intended. By gripping a wire in the correct hole, squeezing tightly, and then working the wire strippers around and around, the insulation can be stripped from the wire without touching the wire itself.

The alternative is to strip wire with a knife. With some practice this works fine, but all to often using a knife results in knicked and thinned wire which can weaken the connection.

Last is the soldering gun ⑦. The one illustrated is a 175-watt electric gun with a tip broad enough to solder light wires together. Hobbyists' soldering guns can also be used, although they tend to be too small for efficient use when making electrical repairs around the home.

PART THREE

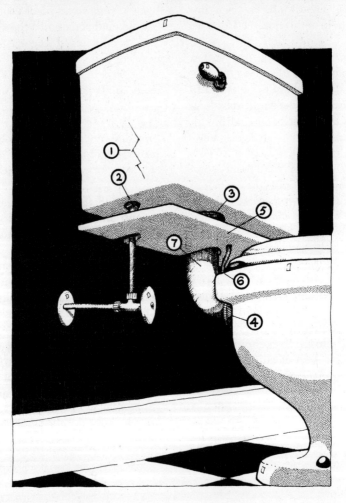

PLUMBING REPAIRS

THE MAIN SUPPLY

Although not as life-threatening as electrical disasters, plumbing disasters can wreak just as much havoc to your house. Consequently, the first rule of plumbing, as with electricity, is to know how to shut it off.

Turning off the water can be a little harder than turning off the electricity for the simple reason that the main valve may be a lot harder to find that the service or fuse box. There is no mistaking a fuse box once you have found it, and one of the switches in or on it is usually marked "on" and "off." Unfortunately, one valve looks pretty much like another, and only rarely are they marked. Add to this the fact that there is usually no time to experiment, turning first one valve and then the next, when water is gushing out in torrents all over the living room floor. And even more confusing is the fact that there may be many other valves which may have nothing at all to do with the water supply, such as heating valves, but which can easily be mistaken for part of the plumbing system.

All of this means that no matter where you live it is an excellent idea to find out where the water supply originates—and how to turn it off—*before* anything goes wrong.

People who live in apartments or houses in urban areas with municipal water supplies ① should look for something called the main gate valve ②. This is usually located either just inside or just outside the house, near the spot where the water line enters the building. If you have a water meter ③, the gate valve may either be a part of the meter—and require a wrench to turn it (so keep one handy, near the meter)—or be a separate valve close to the meter. The meter itself may be underground or, in warm climates like California,

may be found aboveground.

If your house has its own water supply, this will more than likely be a well, usually located somewhere outside—although older houses were often built over a well. The pipe ④ that comes from the well, before going on to supply the house, will first pass through a pressure tank ⑤.

Pressure tanks are now made much smaller than they used to be but old or new they are all basically the same shape. Some are fatter and some are thinner than the one in the illustration, and most will have a few more pipes and gauges attached. The pipe that enters the house and proceeds to the pressure tank is the water line, and will have a shutoff valve in it before it enters the tank. This valve is the main control ⑥. However, with some pressure tanks you will also have the option of turning the water supply off at the point where it leaves the tank ⑦.

Whichever system you have, find the main valve and tag it clearly ⑧ so that it is also obvious to anyone else, in case of an emergency.

If you are going to turn the water off for an extended period of time, it is also advisable to turn off the water heater, for you might damage the water tank if it is heated while empty.

When you know how to turn off the main supply, you are safe. It may well be more convenient, however, to isolate just one part of the plumbing system. For example, most sinks have their own shutoff valves located underneath, and it is not really necessary to turn of the main supply if you just want to work on the sink and its faucets. But whatever your plans, at least know where the main valve is.

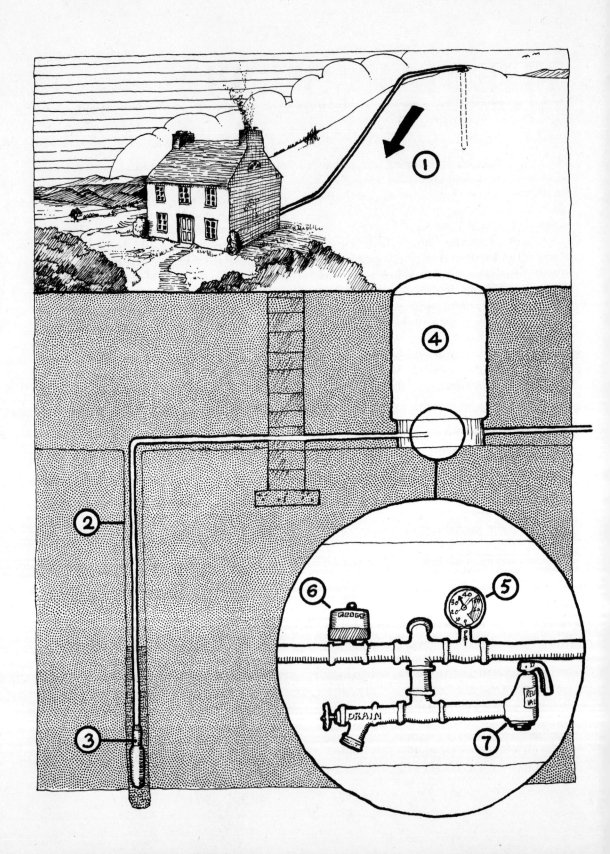

PRESSURE TANK PROBLEMS

Most country and many suburban homes get water from their own wells. Unless you have a gravity-fed system ①, in which the water supply is higher than the house, and all you have to do to get water is to turn the tap on and let it flow out, a well ② will also require a pump ③ and a pressure tank ④.

If you turn the tap and nothing comes out, there are no leaks anywhere, and the pipes are not frozen, the trouble is probably in the well and pressure tank system.

To get the water from the well to the pressure tank requires a pump, which will either be located by the pressure tank or will be a submersible pump at the bottom of the well. Both require electricity to make them work, so the first things to check are that the electricity is on and whether or not a fuse has blown. If the problem is indeed electrical, you should call an electrician—or a plumber, since most plumbers can fix "well electrics."

If there does not appear to be an electrical problem, check the pressure tank. There should be a gauge ⑤ on or near the pressure tank which indicates how much pressure there is in the tank. Most tanks are designed to operate around 40 psi.

The way these work is very simple. The pump sends water from the well into the tank until the air in the tank is compressed by the incoming water to a pressure of forty pounds per square inch—40 psi. When this pressure is reached a switch is triggered that stops the pump. When water is drawn from the tank the pressure drops until at a certain prearranged level, usually around 20 psi, the switch is triggered and the pump starts pumping again.

By looking at the pressure gauge you can tell whether or not there is any water in the tank, and if so how much. If the gauge reads 40 psi you can be sure it is full. If it reads 0 psi, it is empty.

There are various reasons why a tank may lose pressure. Therefore, most are fitted with a reset button ⑥, sometimes called a pressure switch. Most reset buttons are red, and are clearly marked. They provide a way for you to start the pump working and hopefully fill up the tank. Then the tank's own switch should take over when water is drawn out again. All you do is to hold the button down for a few seconds and then release it. You should see the pressure start to rise, and in some cases you can hear the pump working or hear the water running into the tank.

If nothing happens, the well may have run dry. This, however, is usually presaged by the water becoming discolored before drying up. If there was nothing untoward about the color of the water before it disappeared, then either the pump is broken or the switch in the pressure tank is broken. Both problems require professional help.

In case the pump should fail to stop for some reason, a relief valve ⑦ attached to the tank will let water out should the pressure in the tank become excessive. As a further precaution, many submersible pumps will only operate (no matter what the pressure tank is telling them to do) as long as they are submerged—so if the well should run dry, the pump will automatically stop.

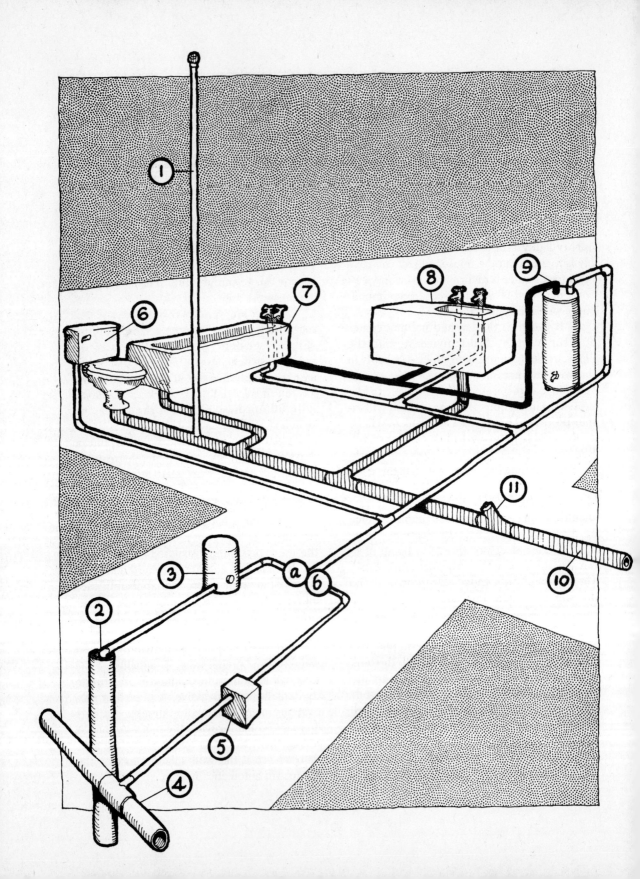

THE PLUMBING SYSTEM

It can be hard to make sense of the maze of pipes that constitute the plumbing system of a house, the more so since much of it is in dark, hard-to-reach places. Consequently, many potentially simple repairs are never attempted. For this reason a very basic system is illustrated here. If you understand the principles—which apply to virtually every domestic plumbing system—as exemplified here, you stand a much better chance of being able to identify the components of your own system.

Each system is tailored to the requirements of a particular house, and so hardly any two houses (except for identical tract houses) will have the same pipes in the same places. But, and this is the key to an understanding of what is going on, they will all have "water in" and "water out." Apart from one or more vent stacks ①, which provide ventilation to the system, all other pipes either bring water to the various fittings around the house or take it away.

Let us look at "water in" first. Whether you have your own well ② and pressure tank ③, or get your water from a municipal water main ④ via a water meter ⑤, a cold water supply will enter the house at Ⓐ or Ⓑ.

The route the cold water supply takes after entering the house may vary, but you should be able to trace the pipe to the toilet ⑥, the tub ⑦, the kitchen sink ⑧, and the water heater ⑨. Water heaters are discussed in more detail elsewhere, but for the moment suffice it to say that a cold water line goes in, and a hot water line comes out. In the illustra-

tion opposite, the hot water line is black. From the hot water heater it runs to the kitchen sink ⑧ and then the tub ⑦.

This, of course, is a very simple system. Most houses have a variety of other fittings that receive water, including laundry sinks, washing machines, washstands in various bathrooms, dishwashers, and outside faucets for garden hoses. There is no fixed rule for the order in which these fittings are plumbed. This is the result of the layout of the house, although well-designed houses often have the plumbing arranged so that it is as compact as possible, with the kitchen and the bathroom back-to-back, for example. It also makes sense to try and keep hot water lines as short as possible so that not too much heat is lost between the heater and the outlet—a problem even if the pipes are insulated.

The other side of the system is the drainage—the "water out" part. All drain pipes, which are shaded in the illustration, and which tend to be larger than supply lines, eventually converge into one large pipe ⑩ that leaves the building to flow into a sewage system of some kind. Only two other pipes leave the drain—the vent stack (or stacks) mentioned earlier ①, and one or more cleanouts ⑪, which are large access plugs from which blockages can be attacked. The exception is the possible use, in more modern buildings, of a secondary drain pipe that carries away "gray water": water with no solid waste in it, such as water from washing machines.

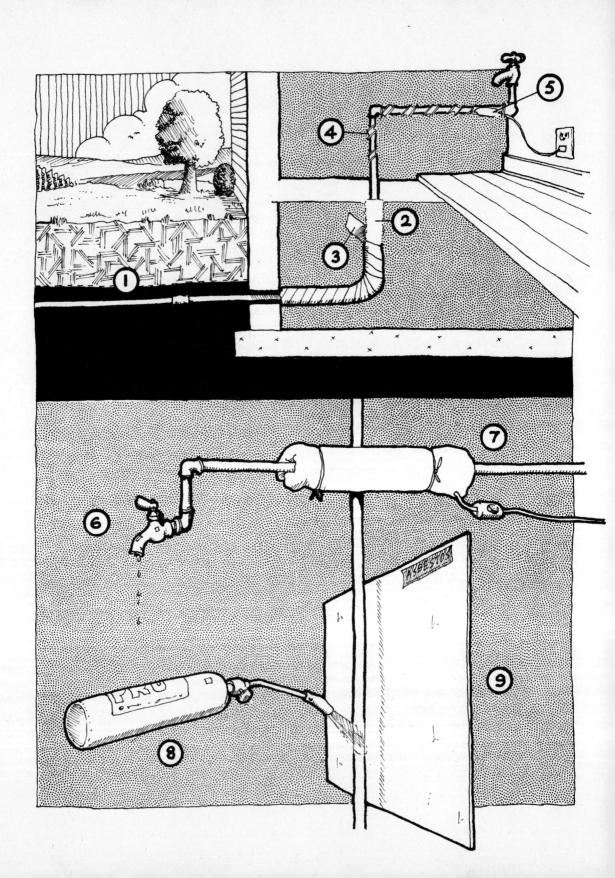

FROZEN PIPES

Plumbing systems in areas where the temperature drops below 32 degrees Fahrenheit should be installed with certain precautions taken against freezing.

All water lines outside the house should be either buried below the frost line ①—the depth to which the ground commonly freezes in winter—or well insulated. This insulation can take the same form as that needed by interior water lines that run through unheated parts of the house, such as cold basements and unheated garages.

Pipes may be wrapped in fiberglass insulation ②—which is available in long narrow rolls for this purpose, and which is then covered with waterproof plastic ③—or they may be fitted with heat-tape ④. Heat-tape is wrapped around the pipe and then plugged into an electric outlet. A thermostat ⑤ built into the tape turns on the heat automatically when required.

Temporary measures against freezing include opening a faucet so that a little water drips continually. This is, of course, extremely wasteful, but since running water freezes more slowly than standing water it can be better than waking up in the morning to find all the pipes frozen—or burst, and leaking even more water.

A light bulb or two kept burning close to exposed pipes during a cold spell can also help. If you find you have a constant need for such temporary measures it would be better to insulate the pipes properly and be able to forget about it.

In the event your pipes do freeze there are several ways to thaw them out. Before you begin, however, take two precautions. Firstly, open the faucet ⑥ nearest the frozen pipe so that vapor from the melting ice will have an escape vent, and secondly, be prepared to shut off the main valve in case the thawed pipe discloses a leak in a burst pipe.

Various forms of heat can be used to thaw the pipes, including electric blankets ⑦ wrapped around the afflicted part, hair driers, warm wet rags, propane torches ⑧, and even welding equipment—though, since it could have dangerous consequences, this should only be attempted by a qualified plumber, although it is often the only way to reach frozen lines that are buried deep in the ground. Providing that you take care not to set fire to the building when using a propane torch, the other methods are safe enough, though sometimes messy.

Remember always to work back from an open faucet so that melted ice can run out. Since water expands when it freezes, the expansion may have burst the pipe, so be on the lookout for leaks.

If you do use a propane torch, be very careful not to let the pipe get too hot, especially around joints and fittings. You might damage them and cause a leak. A sheet of asbestos ⑨ or sheet metal can be useful in protecting adjacent walls in confined areas.

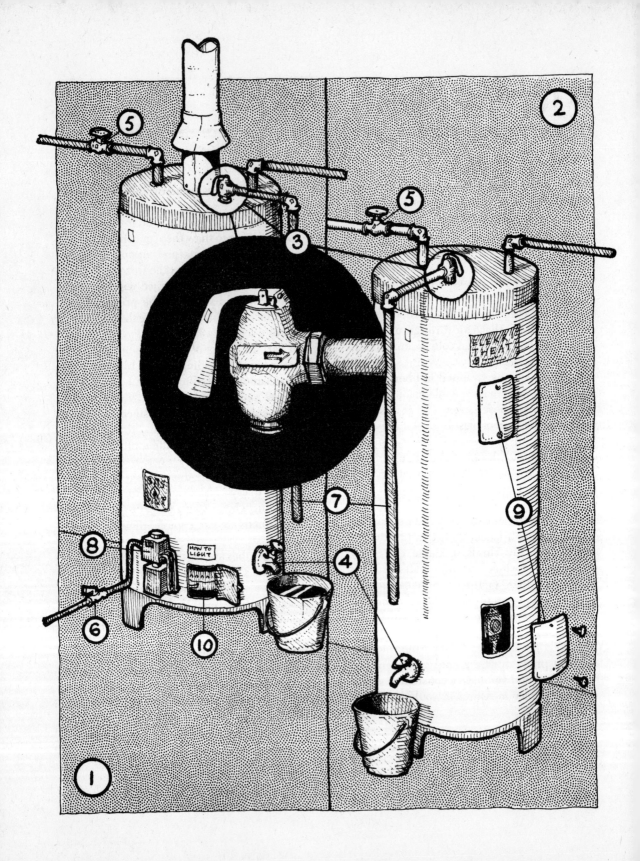

HOT WATER HEATER PROBLEMS

Although various types of solar-powered and refrigeration-hot water systems are now beginning to be used, most are still used in conjunction with the two basic types of discrete water heaters—gas ① or electric ② hot water heaters.

Both types can develop leaks in the same two places: the pressure relief valve ③ and the drain valve ④. If you discover a leak the first thing to do is to shut off the water supply to the heater. There is usually a shutoff value ⑤ in the cold water inlet line just before it enters the tank. Equally importantly, however, *turn off the heat*. If gas, turn off the gas inlet valve ⑥, and if electric, turn off the heater switch or cut off the power to the heater at the service box.

Having shut off the power (and the heat), investigate the leak. If the leak was in the pressure relief valve you can try moving its lever up and down a little to see if doing so reseats it and stops the leak. Bear in mind that the valve's job is precisely to leak (when necessary), and that preventing it from being able to leak is dangerous. If it leaks badly it should be replaced. You could, however, see that it is fitted with a runoff pipe ⑦ to carry away any water that does leak out safely.

Drain valves ④ often leak when they are used after a long period of not having been used. Manufacturers recommend that you open this valve a couple of times a year to drain off any sediment that may have collected in the tank—as soon as the water runs clear, shut the valve again. But if this has not been done for a while, a sudden opening can lead to a chronic leak, since the valve may have seated itself so firmly that opening it may break the seal. Since replacement is a costly job, if you have not performed this little bit of maintenance in the last two years it is probably better to leave this valve alone.

If the leak is elsewhere than in these two valves, the chances are that the whole tank needs replacing. Your only course of action will be to drain the whole tank, not forgetting to turn off the heat.

If gas heaters produce water that is too hot, the cure is simple—turn down the thermostat ⑧. If electric heaters are producing excessively hot water do the same thing—but remember that there are often two thermostat controls, and that they are usually hidden behind access panels ⑨, unlike the single exposed thermostat found on gas heaters.

With an electric heater, no hot water usually means that a fuse has blown or the power is off. Check all the switches and the relevant circuit in the service box before you call the electrician.

No hot water from a gas heater is invariably the result of either having run out of gas (which can happen if you have your own gas tanks rather than obtain it from a municipal supply) or the pilot light having gone out. If there is still gas, check the pilot light orifice ⑩ to see that it is clean, check for drafts that may have blown the light out, and relight the pilot according to the directions (usually printed nearby).

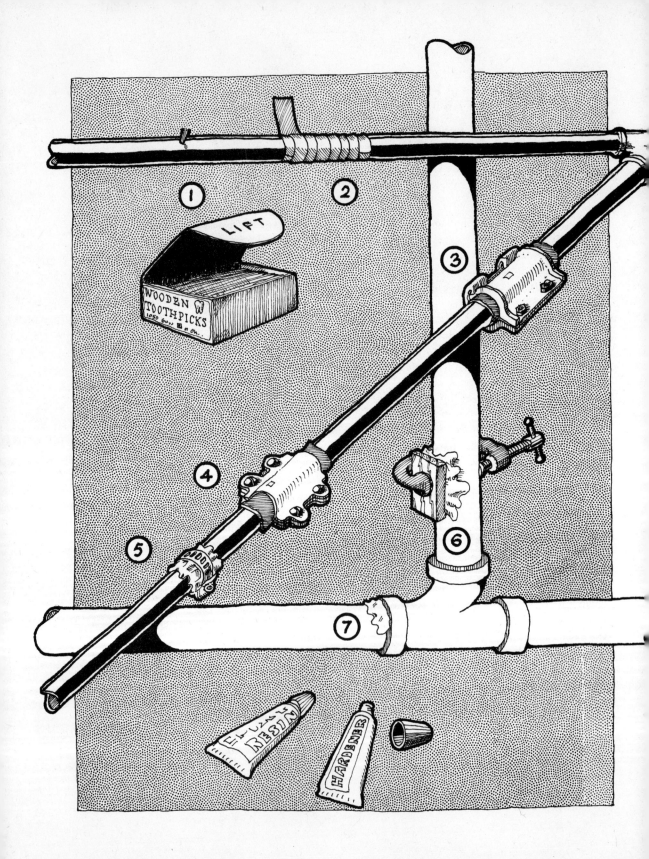

LEAKY PIPES

A leaky pipe is the kind of emergency that typically happens when there is little hope of outside help. Although the results can be disastrous if unchecked, the cure is usually quite simple, and quickly effected.

The first thing to do is to cut off the water supply to that part of the plumbing—if you are unsure of how to do this, turn off the main supply valve (see page 91). Do this even if the leak is merely a drip and not actually gushing out because almost all repairs call for dry pipes.

If it is just a pinhole-size leak you can try forcing a toothpick ① into the hole, breaking off the end and wrapping the toothpick in place with tape. The idea here is that the water will swell the wood of the toothpick and close the leak.

Small leaks can also be stopped by wrapping electrical tape ② around them. But for the tape to adhere properly the pipe must be dry to start with. Overlap each turn of the tape at least half its width and apply at least three layers.

Larger leaks can be stopped with sleeve clamps ③, ④, and ⑤. There are several methods to use here. Hardware stores sell metal sleeves made to fit around different size pipes. A piece of rubber (such as from an old inner tube) is clamped under the sleeve and then the sleeve is tightened down. There are various designs of sleeves—some that hinge ③ and some that are screwed down on both sides ④. The only important thing is that you use the right size sleeve for the job.

A common hose clamp ⑤ can be pressed into service as a sleeve clamp for small leaks; the most useful sizes for residential water lines are numbers 16 and 12.

If you are forced to improvise, a lot can be done with a simple C-clamp and a rag held in place with a block of wood ⑥. Be careful not to crush the pipe when you tighten the clamp.

When leaks occur at joints it is even more important to drain the pipe before attempting any repair. None of the cures will work on wet pipes, and if you are attempting to sweat a joint in copper pipe (see page 127) you could create dangerous steam pressure inside the pipe if it is still full of water.

One simple repair at a joint that can be permanent involves the use of epoxy ⑦. This commonly comes in the form of a tube containing resin and a tube containing hardener. Simply mix equal parts and spread it around the joint. Within a few hours it will have hardened sufficiently to withstand normal household water pressure.

When leaks occur in threaded pipes (see page 125) very often just tightening the pipe with a wrench, while holding the other part firmly with another wrench, will stop the leak. Do not attempt to turn the pipe too much, for screwing in one end necessarily screws out the other end. If this happens you will have to disassemble the whole section and start again from scratch (as described on page 125). A slight twist, however, may often solve the problem.

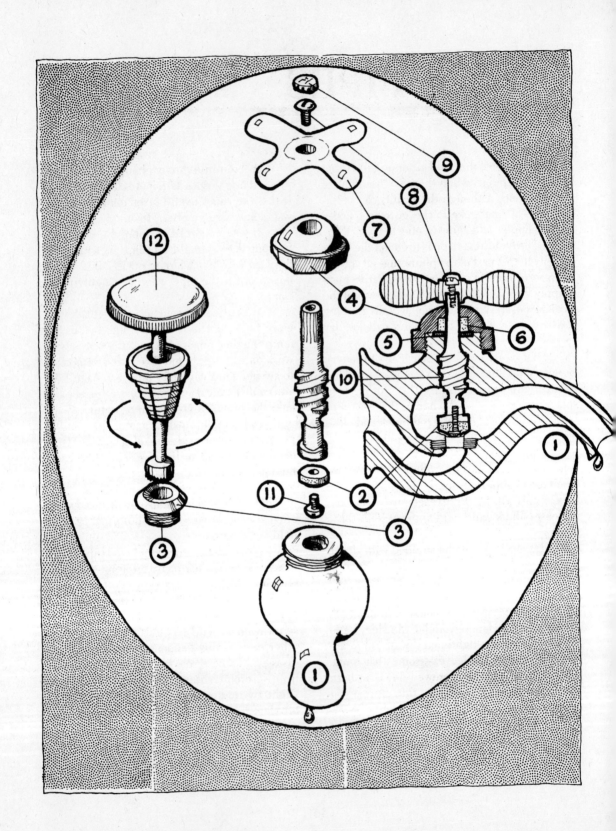

DRIPPING FAUCET

All faucets can be divided into two types: faucets with washers and washerless faucets. The simplification stops there, however, because there is an enormous variety of both types. The more modern washerless faucets often seem to have been designed to make disassembly by the uninitiated as difficult as possible, since the various nuts and screws that hold the things together are usually very hard to find, being hidden under snap caps for example.

Nevertheless, drips usually emanate from one of only three locations, and being able to tell which kind of drip you have can lessen the frustration of attempting to disassemble the wrong part.

If water drips out of the spout ① no matter how hard you turn the tap, the washer ② or its seat ③ is worn. If water leaks out of the base of the handle, the packing nut ④ is either loose or its washer ⑤ or packing material ⑥ is worn. If water appears at the base of the faucet, then the coupling nut, which connects the plumbing to the faucet under the sink, is defective.

Without a special tool called a basin wrench it can be very hard to rectify the last type of leak. Moreover, since an effective repair may involve disconnecting the pipe completely in order to replace the washers, this job is probably best left to a professional. The first two leaks, however, can be tackled with little more than a screwdriver and a common adjustable wrench, and success depends not on equipment but an understanding of how

the basic washer faucet works.

First of all, before you start to disassemble the faucet, remember to turn the water off. There should be a shutoff valve in the line below the sink or close to the faucet, but if you can't find it, or if the water still leaks from the faucet after it has been turned off, then turn off the water at the main supply valve (see page 91).

The first job is to remove the tap or handle ⑦. The screw ⑧ that holds this on may be visible or it may be hidden under a decorative cap ⑨. Next, possibly also hidden under a decorative housing, is the packing nut ④. If this is the source of your leak, tightening it may cure the problem. Alternatively, it may need a new washer.

When the packing nut is removed you can screw the handle back on and by turning it as if you were turning the water on, the valve stem ⑩ will come out. At the bottom of the valve stem you will see the washer ②, which is screwed in place by a small brass screw ⑪. When replacing the washer, be sure to use a new washer that is the right size. To make this easier, hardware stores sell small assortments that usually contain the one you want.

The part against which the washer is compressed when the faucet is shut off is known as the valve seat ③, and this should be smooth. If it is knicked or worn it should either be replaced (some can be screwed out) or made smooth with a reseater kit ②—a cheap tool which is screwed into the stem aperture and simply twisted around for a few times.

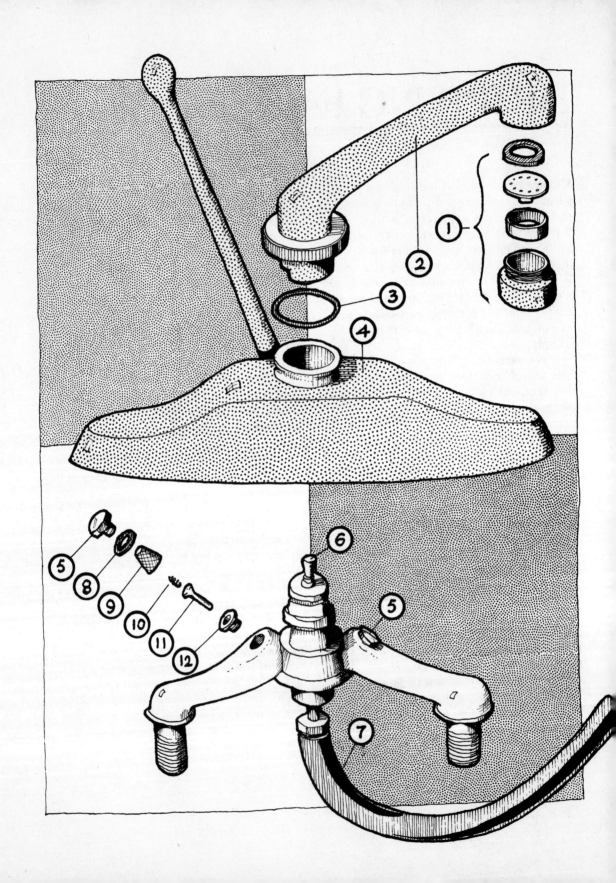

CLOGGED FAUCET

If less water seems to be coming out of the faucet than previously, and you are sure the well is not running dry and that all shutoff valves—the main one and any in the various water lines that lead to whichever faucet is giving trouble—are wide open, and if, moreover, the water pressure appears undiminished in other parts of the house, then you are probably suffering one of the disadvantages of "progress." Most modern faucets, especially those found in kitchens and bathrooms, are equipped with aerators—little screw-on devices at the mouth of the spout—whose purpose is to make the water flow out of the spout in a nice neat stream.

Since they work by only allowing the water to pass through a number of small holes, they are subject to being clogged up by very small particles of grit or lime that might otherwise flow right on through.

Faucets that are controlled by a lever, mixing hot and cold water, can also become clogged as a result of the small strainers (which form part of the control assembly) gathering grit and debris.

The illustration shows an exploded view of a mixer-type faucet with an aerator in the spout. Remember that all types of faucets may have aerators, and these are the first thing to check when the water flow slows to a trickle.

To remove the aerator ① can be quite difficult if it is screwed in tightly. Nothing seems to grip it until it has become scratched and gouged by fruitless effort. To avoid this, make sure it is completely dry and then wrap some tape around it to protect the finish. Now use a pair of pliers or vise-grips if you have them. When replacing the unit, smear a little petroleum jelly on the threads to make removal easier next time.

Once it is off the spout, be careful to disassemble the aerator so that you can remember the order in which the parts fit together. Not all models are exactly the same, and it is very easy to reassemble them backwards so that they work even worse than before!

To clean the strainer in mixer faucets you must turn the water off and remove the spout ②, under which is an O-ring ③ that should be replaced if the spout was leaking around its base.

Once the spout and its O-ring are off, the escutcheon housing ④ may be lifted off to reveal the plugs ⑤ that contain the valve assemblies, and the diverter assembly ⑥ (this is discussed on the following page). Unscrewing the plug will disclose a small washer ⑧, and the strainer ⑨, which should be cleaned of all sediment. If you progress further, you'll find a small spring ⑩, which you should be careful not to lose, the valve stem ⑪, and finally the valve seat ⑫. This can also become clogged, but it is sometimes hard to remove without a special Allen key (although sometimes a long thin screwdriver will do the job is you are careful not to damage anything).

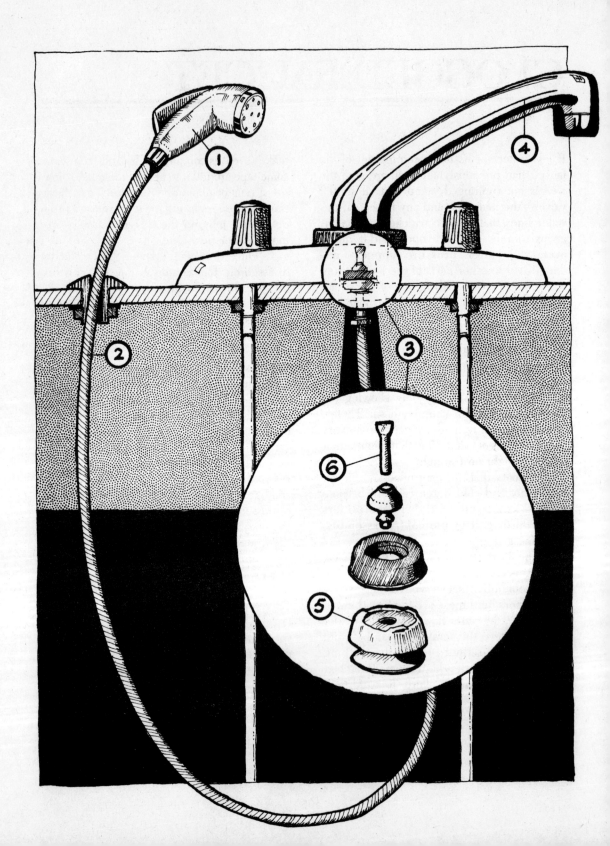

FAUCET SPRAY TROUBLE

Many kitchen sinks are now equipped with a thumb-control spray ①, attached by a hose ②—which passes through the top of the sink, usually at the side of the faucets—to the underneath of the faucet unit.

The heart of the system is a small device known as a diverter valve ③, which is normally housed immediately below the swinging spout ④. When all is well, there is water in the spray hose right up to the thumb control. When you turn a faucet, water flows out of the spout, but if you depress the thumb control, water runs out of the hose. In doing so, the water pressure on the diverter valve is changed and a piston-like unit ⑤ snaps down shutting off most if not all of the water supply to the faucet spout. When you release the thumb control, the previous water pressure is restored, the piston moves up and again, and water flows through the spout.

Leaks may develop where the spray is connected to the hose and where the hose is connected to the faucet unit. The latter leak can usually be cured by tightening the nut that holds the hose to the faucet; the former is not always curable since the spray heads are commonly made in one piece with the hose—the idea being that you will have to buy a whole new hose. This may be necessary in the event that the hose is kinked, worn, frayed, or otherwise leaking. Do not forget to turn off the water supply to the faucet unit before you disconnect the hose or you will get wet.

If no water comes out of the spray inspect the aerator in the spout of the faucet (as described in the previous section). If this is blocked, water will not divert. A quick test is to remove the aerator and then operate the spray—if it works, the problem is in the aearator.

The next place to check is the nozzle of the spray itself. This can also become clogged. If you can't get it off to clean it, use a small pin to clean the spray holes.

If there is still no water from the spray, inspect the hose for leaks or kinks. The hose sometimes gets caught up in the pipes under the sink, and you should check to see that it hangs freely and can be pulled up through the sink without binding anywhere.

The last place to look is at the diverter valve itself. It is reached by unscrewing the ring, nut, or collar that holds the spout down and pulling the whole thing up. Underneath, usually sitting in a little puddle of water, will be the diverter valve. Before replacing it with a new one, try jiggling the stem ⑥—it sometimes gets stuck as a result of small pieces of sediment in the water supply. Alternatively, pull the whole thing out, replace the spout, turn on the water to flush the pipes for a moment, then replace the valve and see if it is working.

In the event that none of the above works you will have to replace the diverter valve, but here is a piece of good news: the replacement parts are standardized so that no matter what the brand, you should have no trouble obtaining a new one to fit. When you put it in just be sure that the stem ⑥ is pointing up.

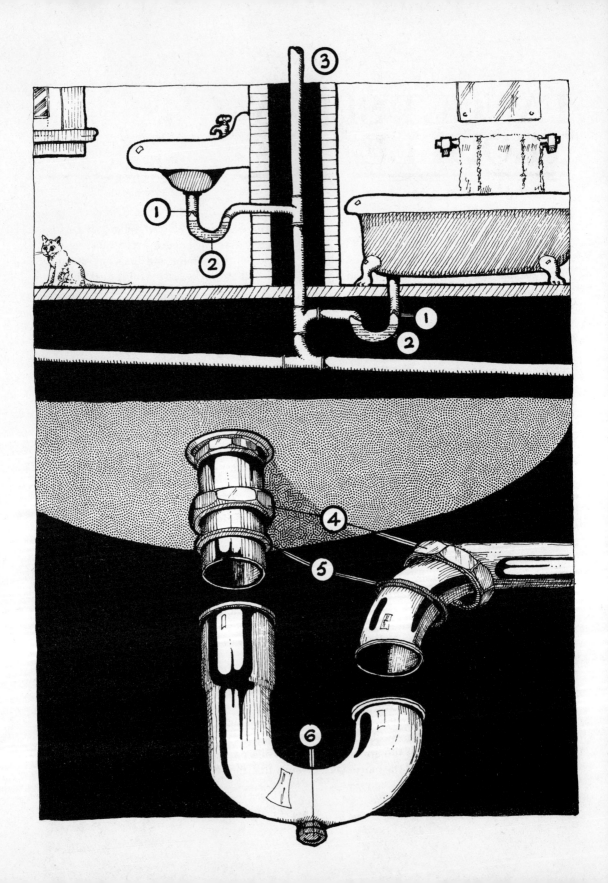

THE SINK TRAP

When water drains out of a sink (or a tub or a toilet), before it enters the drainage pipes proper it first passes through a contorted section of pipe known variously as a P-trap, U-trap, S-trap, or simply trap ①. The chief purpose of the trap, besides forming a convenient way to connect the fixture to the drain pipes and providing a convenient place from which to gain access to possible blockages, is to provide a water barrier ② to the noxious sewer gases that might otherwise rise up the drain pipes and pervade the house. The trap, therefore, both traps water in the pipes and traps the sewer gases (which should then be forced to rise up through the stack vent ③— see also page 119).

This clever piece of plumbing, because of its very necessary contorted shape and consequent extra joints, can become both clogged or leaky—both of which can create an unpleasant emergency. Although traps under tubs and toilets can be rather difficult to get to, working on them is essentially the same as working on sink traps.

If a trap is leaking, try tightening the slip nuts ④ that hold the U-shaped section to the other parts. Be careful to wrap something protective around the nuts before you apply a wrench or you may damage the chrome finish. If tightening does not help, then the washers ⑤ probably need replacing. Older traps have rubber washers which tend to dry out and crumble away; newer traps are fitted with plastic washers—these are much better, but be sure to get the right size: if they are not exactly the correct diameter they will not work.

At the bottom of most traps is a cleanout plug ⑥. If this has not been touched in a long time you may be unable to make it waterproof when you replace it, so be prepared to give it a new washer if you do unscrew it. Should it be rusted at all, clean off the threads with a wire brush and then coat them with a liberal amount of joint compound—which can be bought in small tubes at hardware stores. The joint compound both helps to prevent future rust and seal the plug.

The only other connection that might leak is where the trap is joined to the underneath of the sink. This is not a common leak since the fitting in the base of the sink normally runs down inside the trap a little way. It is dangerous to attempt to tighten this connection too vigorously because you may break the seal around the sink outlet.

When a sink becomes blocked there are several courses of action, one of which is to clean the trap. If you decide on the trap approach, begin by unscrewing the cleanout plug ⑥, bearing in mind the caution above. Remember to have a bucket handy underneath, and if the blockage does not immediately gush out, poke a wire coat hanger, with a little hook bent into the end, up both sides of the trap. If this does not produce results, undo the slip nuts and remove the U section completely to make sure it is absolutely clean. This is the place where sink blockages most commonly occur. You should always attempt a manual cleaning before resorting to chemical cleaners, since the corrosive nature of these cleaners makes them potentially damaging to both you and the plumbing.

If the trap is clean and the sink still will not drain when the trap is reconnected and the sink refilled, turn to the next section.

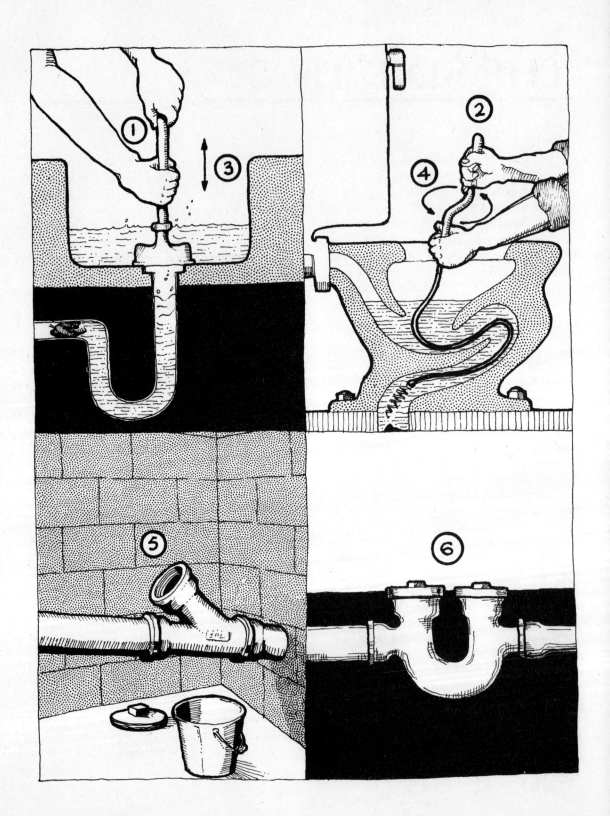

BLOCKED DRAINS

A toilet that will no longer flush as fast as before and which threatens to spill out over the floor, a bathtub that will not drain away, and a sink left full of dirty water even though the plug is out are all problems that happen to everyone sooner or later.

If after having made sure that the plug hole and any strainer basket that the sink or tub might be equipped with is clear, and if after having checked that the trap is clean (as explained in the previous section), the water still stands, it is time to use a little deductive reasoning to locate the blockage, and get out the plumber's friend ① (also known as a force cup or plunger), and the plumber's snake ② (also known as a drain auger).

If only one fixture will not drain, then you know that the blockage is in the drainpipe that connects that fixture to the remainder of the house's plumbing; but if several fixtures will not drain, then you know that the blockage is further along. If nothing will drain, then the blockage must be between the last fixture and the main drain or the septic tank, if the house has one. This last possibility also raises the question of whether or not the septic tank itself is full and backing up.

But to proceed in an orderly manner: if only one fixture is blocked and everything else drains freely, the chances are good that you can free the drain with vigorous use of the plunger. For the plunger to be effective it must be operated in four or five inches of water—any overflow hole must be stopped up (with a handy rag). Center the plunger cup over the drain hole and push down violently ③. The air in the cup forces the water against the blockage, and, even more effectively, creates a powerful suction action as it is released. Repeat this continuously for at least five min-

utes—if necessary.

If the plunger does not do the trick, and if more than one fixture is blocked, a snake may be necessary—since this can reach much further. There are various sorts, from simple lengths of wire with hooks, to sophisticated versions with cranking handles, sheathed cables, and large corkscrews on the end. But the principle behind all of them is the same: insert the snake and keep turning. The turning helps the snake negotiate sharp bends—such as exist in a toilet bowl ④. When resistance is felt, keep turning (in an attempt to hook into the blockage) and slowly withdraw the snake—while still turning. If you use up the entire snake without encountering any resistance, get a longer snake—they are made up to 50 feet in length.

If everything in the house is blocked up, start from the other end. Just before the main drain leaves the house—as every drain must do—there should be a cleanout plug ⑤ or housetrap ⑥. These are meant to be opened in the event of a blockage to allow access with an auger, but beware! If everything in the house is undrained, there could be a lot of water waiting to rush out of the cleanout when it is opened, so be prepared with mops and buckets.

If everything runs out of the house trap but things back up again when it is closed and more water is used, then there is either something wrong with the municipal drain or your septic tank. Although the septic tank should have an inspection port into which you can peer to double check that the tank is indeed full, you can be pretty sure at this point that the problem is now out of your hands and it is time to call in professional help. (For more on septic tanks see page 117.)

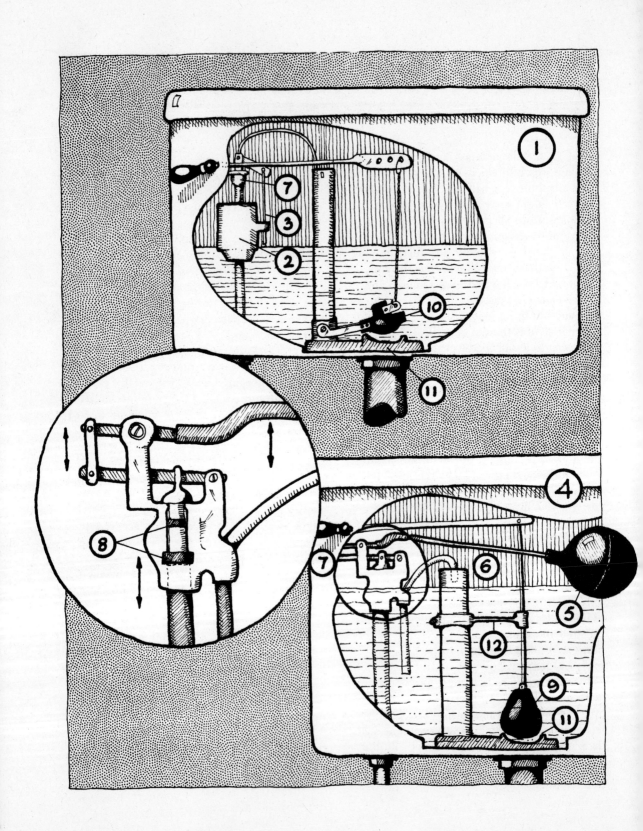

TOILET TANK PROBLEMS

Although designs vary from manufacturer to manufacturer, there are only two basic types of toilet tank flushing mechanisms.

The newer kind ① is made of plastic, and consists of a float ② that rides up and down a rod ③. Until the float reaches the very top of the rod, the water refilling the tank (after each flush) is allowed in at full force. When the tank is full, it then shuts off quickly, all at once. This results in a quicker, quieter, and more reliable action than the other type ④, which relies on a float ball ⑤ at the end of an arm ⑥. In this case the float ball directly controls the water inlet valve ⑦, and shuts it down bit by bit during the whole time that the ball is rising, until the water inlet is completely shut off at the end of the ball's rise.

There are three reasons why the toilet may not stop running. One has to do with the inlet valve ⑦, another may be caused by a faulty float ball ⑤, or its more modern counterpart, the plastic float ②, and the last is a problem with the device that shuts off the flow into the toilet bowl.

The inlet valve, which is opened when the tank is flushed, and closed by either the plastic float or the float ball when the tank is full again, relies on rubber, fiber, or plastic washers ⑧ to effect a complete seal. If you can hold the plastic float or the float ball up, and water still comes through the inlet valve, it either needs new washers, or, more easily done but more expensive, it needs to be replaced. In areas of hard water, sediment some-times forms and prevents the perfect operation of this valve. Jiggling it up and down by hand sometimes helps.

If the plastic float or the float ball does not rise high enough, it will not shut off the inlet valve. The newer plastic float must then be replaced, but the older float ball can sometimes be bent down on its rod so that it shuts off the inlet valve at a lower level. If either leak, they should be replaced.

When the toilet is flushed, a trip lever removes a device that controls entry of water into the bowl. This device may be either a rubber ball ⑨ on the end of a rod or chain, or a plastic flapper ⑩. As the water flows into the tank again these devices should settle back over the inlet ⑪ and completely seal it. If they are misaligned or worn and leaky, water will continually flow into the bowl. This will be evidenced by continuous ripples on the surface of the water in the bowl and a possible singing of the inlet valve as it attempts in vain to fill up the tank. Misalignment can usually be corrected by the proper bending of the various guide rods ⑫, but wear is remedied only by replacement.

The opposite problem—of not enough water—is usually the result of a partially blocked inlet valve. Try jiggling it to remove any sediment. If this fails, replace it—but first check that the plastic float or float ball is dropping when the tank is flushed (and so opening the inlet valve properly).

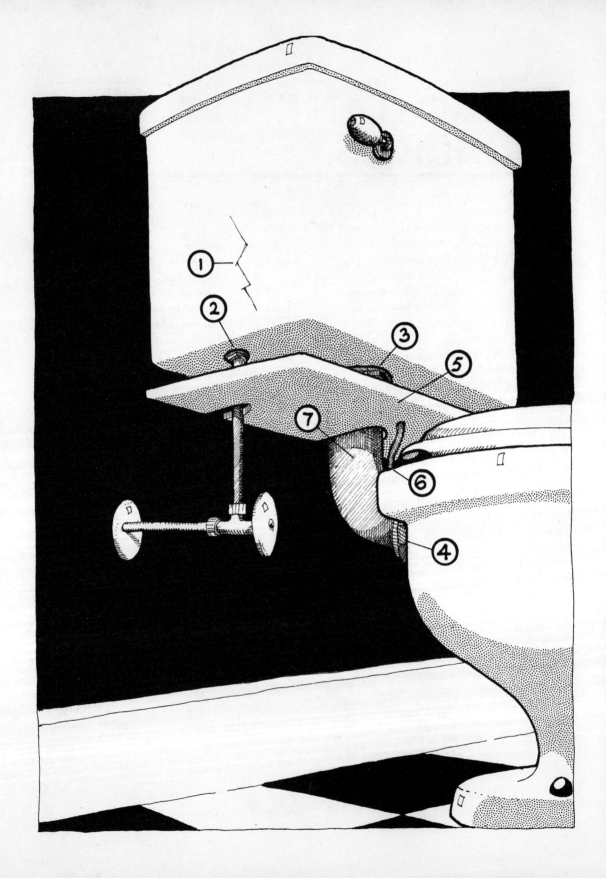

WET TOILET TANK

Water on the *outside* of a toilet tank or reservoir is either the result of a leak or condensation. Check for leaks first.

If the leak is from a crack ① in the bowl or reservoir you will probably want to replace the fixture for the sake of its looks, even though it is possible to seal the leak with one of various compounds available at plumbing supply houses. If the porcelain is intact, however, look at one of the only three places that are likely to leak. These are where the cold water line ② enters the tank or reservoir; where the water leaves the tank on its way to the bowl ③; and where the pipe that carries the water from the tank to the bowl enters the bowl ④. (This pipe is known as the spud pipe.) The leak may be a result of the large nuts which hold the pipes in place being too lose. A *careful* tightening of these nuts, with a large wrench, may help. Too vigorous an effort, however, can do more harm than good, so be careful. What may have happened is that the washers in these joints may have dried up and become brittle—thus no longer providing an effective seal. Unless you are prepared to replace everything, and are equipped with some large plumber's wrenches, call for professional help.

If the water looks more like the result of condensation than a leak, i.e., if it appears higher up the tank than any of the joints just mentioned, and seems to start in a neat horizontal line coincident with the interior water level, then the problem is the result of the water supply being too cold!

If you ignore this problem, which may be chronic, the constant wetness could eventually cause quite a lot of serious damage including raised tiles and rotted floor boards and joists. The easiest solution is to install a special tank tray ⑤—under the tank—which is equipped with a small hose ⑥ that leads into the toilet bowl. The trays are made to be bolted to the spud pipe ⑦. All you have to do is to see that they are properly tilted so that the water they collect is led off into the little hose.

Not all toilets have spud pipes, however, and a better solution may be to drain the tank and make sure the inside is thoroughly dry, and then line it with styrofoam or foam rubber—gluing the insulation to the sides of the tank with an epoxy resin. Make sure that you do not interfere with the flushing mechanism, but cover well up above the water line.

A third solution is to have the plumber tap into a nearby hot water line and install an automatic mixing valve, by warming up the water that goes to the tank so that the condensation no longer occurs.

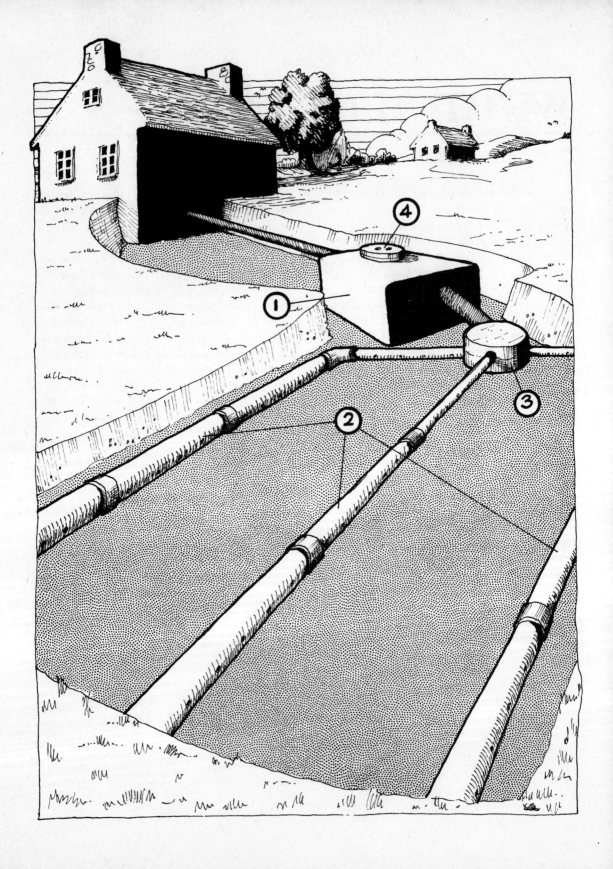

SEPTIC TANK BACKUP

For people who live in urban areas, drainage problems should end at the municipal sewer, but for the millions of people who live in rural and many suburban areas, the final disposition of their house's waste is their own responsibility.

In the vast majority of cases, this is achieved with a septic tank and drainage field. An older method, employing the use of a cesspool—simply a covered pit with porous sides—is being increasingly forbidden by local health authorities since it is unsanitary and inefficient.

The first sign that something is wrong with a septic tank system is usually a bad smell. If the smell is noticeable outdoors it means that the drainage field is saturated or broken. If the smell occurs indoors, and is accompanied by sporadic bubbling when the toilet is flushed, then a full septic tank is indicated.

A description of how the system works will expose the problems which may be encountered, and their prevention. The septic tank ① is a large metal or concrete container buried just below ground, into which the house's waste drains. On entering the tank, the solids separate from the liquids and settle to the bottom where they are gradually broken down by bacterial action. The liquid is drained off from the top of the tank and is leached out into the ground through a system of porous pipes ②. Unfortunately, this is not a balanced system, for sooner or later there will be such an accumulation of solid waste which cannot be further broken down that the tank will become filled to capacity and will have to be pumped out. There are, however, several things that can be done to delay this day.

First, a concrete tank will last infinitely longer than a metal tank, so if your tank has deteriorated to the point of needing replacement, install a concrete one. Second, the size of the tank should be large enough to accommodate the proposed use. Local health codes often stipulate the minimum size allowable, usually on the basis of how many bathrooms and bedrooms a house has; but it makes sense to use the largest possible. Third, what you put into the tank will affect its life. You do not want to inhibit or dilute the bacterial action which makes the tank work, so take care not to flush solids or too much grease down the drain. Feeding the tank once in a while with a spoonful of yeast will ensure that as much material as possible is broken down, and assiduous avoidance of nonbiodegradable detergents will also postpone the day it will have to be pumped out. In addition, large volumes of waste water, such as from washing machines and gutters, should never be led into the septic tank, but into a separate system where they will not dilute the tank's efficiency.

The drainage or disposal field is also important. If it smells, it is a sure indication that the field is not large enough and that an additional junction box ③ with more lines should be installed. How much depends on the porosity of the soil. Once installed, it is only common sense to prevent heavy equipment from driving over the buried pipes to avoid crushing them and destroying the drainage pattern.

With ordinary use an acceptable system may need pumping out every three or four years, but in any event it is wise to perform an inspection periodically through the special cover built into the top of all tanks ④.

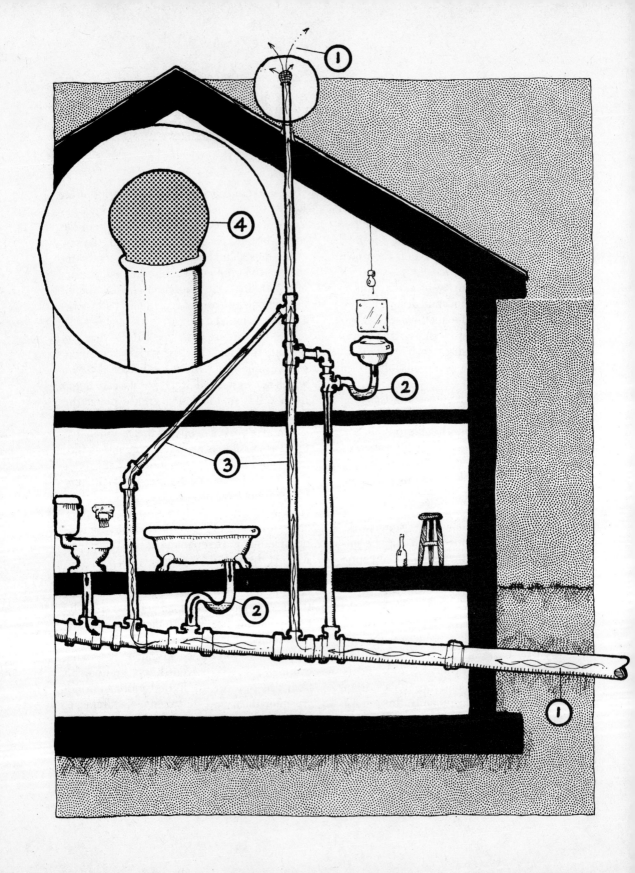

SMELLY PLUMBING

Sewer gases ①, once smelled, are unmistakable the next time you smell them. While less likely in an urban situation where houses are serviced by large municipal sewers, they can still be experienced there as well as in houses that have their own septic tanks. The gases are an unavoidable by-product of the decomposition that takes place as bacteria break down the solid waste in a household's drainage system. Being lighter than air, the gases tend to rise, which means that their most natural path is back up the drains and into the house. This is why most plumbing fixtures are fitted with traps ② (see page 109) in an effort to block the entry of the noxious gases into the house. As a further precaution, most plumbing systems are fitted also with one or more vent stacks ③, whose purpose is to provide an escape route for the gases when they find their upward path through the various plumbing fixtures blocked by the water barriers in the traps.

Ideally there should be a vent stack immediately before every trap, although several vents may be joined into one before actually leaving the house (usually through the roof); at the very least there should be a vent stack coming off the main drain just before it leaves the house.

To be most effective the vent stack should be as vertical as possible and should exit high enough above the roof to be free of any possible downdraft effect. Finally, the top of the stack (or stacks) should be fitted with wire caps ④ to prevent the unwanted entrance of various small creatures, such as birds building nests, since even if they can stand the smell you won't be able to.

Bearing all this in mind, if bad-smelling bubbles start to gurgle up through the toilet or the sink you can be fairly certain that something is amiss with the vent stack.

The first thing to do is to check that, indeed, something has not blocked the top of the stack. If there is no wire cap on top of the stack it is possible that something has become stuck in the pipe. There are two ways to deal with this. You can either use a plumber's snake (see page 111), which is easy to operate but which you might not have on hand, at least not in a length long enough to do the job, or a common garden hose. To use the hose for dislodging any possible blockage insert the hose very carefully into the pipe, a little bit at a time, since it can become kinked very easily. When it will go no further it is probably at the blockage. Having previously set the nozzle on the hose to deliver the most powerful jet of water the hose is capable of, turn on the water quickly for several short blasts—but beware!—water can quickly fill up the pipe and back up through various plumbing fixtures throughout the house and cause further disaster. Have help standing by to alert you in case this should happen.

When all is clear and clean, make sure it doesn't happen again by fitting a proper wire cap on the top of the stack (or stacks).

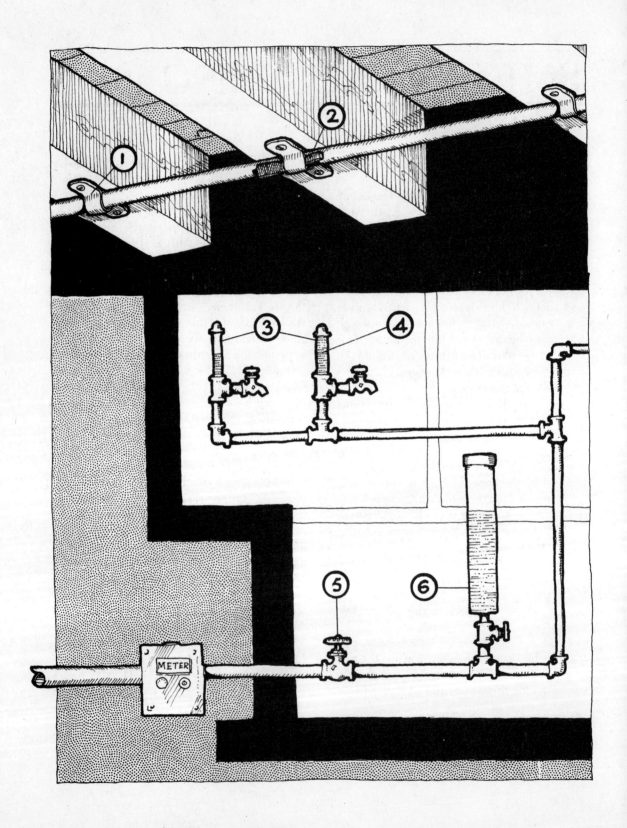

NOISY PLUMBING

While less offensive than smelly plumbing, noisy plumbing can be distinctly alarming, and unexpected onslaughts of the condition known as water hammer or pipe hammer can sound like the clarion calls of catastrophic emergency.

Actually there are several reasons for noisy plumbing. One of the simplest and easiest problems to cure is the result of loosely fixed pipes. Water rushing (or even merely running) through unsecured pipes can cause the pipes to vibrate and bang against adjacent surfaces and other pipes. All that need be done is to trace the course of all exposed pipes and make sure that they are securely supported by brackets or clamps ①, wedging pieces of rubber or felt ② between the pipes and the brackets if need be.

Water hammer is less a clattering, vibrating kind of noise than it is a hard banging noise, usually noticed when a faucet is closed. It is, in fact, caused by the sudden stopping of the water flow in pipes bereft of any cushion of air that causes the knocking—as the water slams into unyielding pipes.

A well-plumbed house has short lengths of pipe ③ extending past the various faucets which are supposed to contain the air which acts as a cushion to prevent water hammer. It sometimes happens that these lengths become filled with water ④ and no longer serve as air cushions. To remedy this situation close the main supply valve ⑤ (see page 91) and then open all of the faucets in the house to drain the entire system. This includes draining the hot water tank as well (remember to turn off the heat). When no more water runs out anywhere, air will have reentered the system. You can then close all the faucets and reopen the main supply valve.

Even with air cushions water hammer may still persist if the water pressure is unusually high. There are two ways to combat this. The easiest thing to do is to close the main supply valve a little and see if this has any effect. A more permanent solution would be to have a plumber install a pressure-reduction valve. This has the advantage of reducing the excess pressure (and thereby eliminating the fearful water hammer) without diminishing the actual volume of water.

In the event that your plumbing system had been put together without air cushions, you do not have to tear the whole lot out and start again. It is possible to install a master air chamber ⑥, which should take care of the whole system, or alternatively, to install copper coil air chambers that are connected under individual sinks, with a minimum of work.

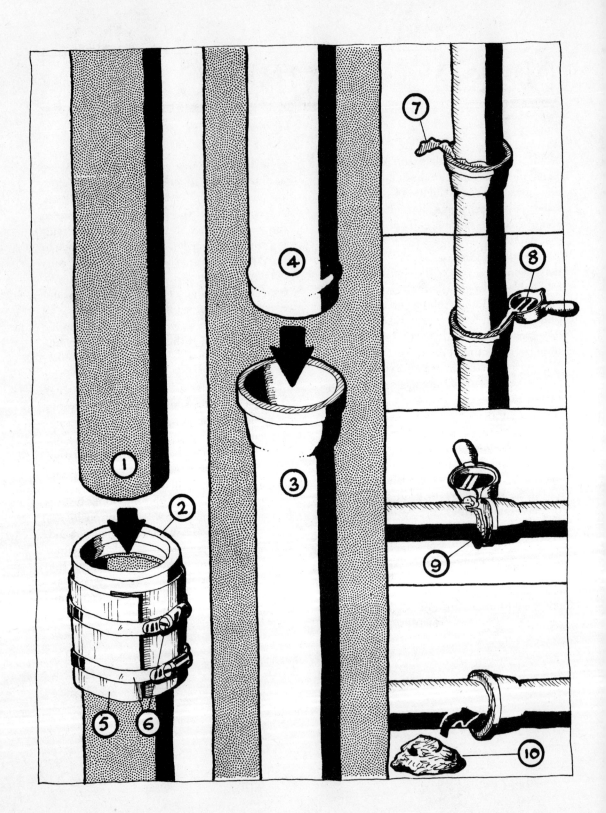

CAST-IRON PIPES

Although various types of plastic pipes have become very popular, many building codes specify the use of cast-iron pipes for particular parts of the plumbing. Cast iron is almost always required for the last length of drain pipe, whether it runs into a municipal sewer or into your own septic tank, and, indeed, many drain systems are all cast iron.

Although it is heavy, not as easy to work with as plastic, and expensive, cast iron has much to recommend it. It is very strong, it lasts a long time, and seldom needs repair. However, situations do occur, from time to time, when it becomes necessary to do more than just put on a temporary clamp (see page 101) to stop a small leak.

The replacement of a section of cast-iron pipe, or the repacking of a hubbed joint, is not difficult, and can turn a situation that might have been an emergency into no more than a (possibly interesting) chore.

Cast-iron pipe, which usually comes in 5-foot lengths, may either have plain ends ① and be joined together with a clamped-on neoprene sleeve ②, or be made with one end in the form of a cup—called a hub ③—into which fits the other end—called the spiggot ④—which is made with a slight ridge around it.

Hubless pipe is joined by simply bringing the two ends close together, and slipping them into a neoprene sleeve, which is then wrapped around with a stainless steel band shield ⑤. Band clamps ⑥ are then screwed tightly over the top.

However, this is not always allowed. Some codes require that only hubbed pipe be used. Hubbed pipe is joined by slipping the spiggot of one pipe into the hub of the other. A layer of oakum ⑦ is packed firmly around the hub, and then the joint is sealed with an inch of molten lead or lead wool.

If molten lead ⑧ is used it sometimes requires the use of a special joint runner ⑨ when horizontal lengths are being worked on. Lead wool ⑩, which looks just like wire wool, but which is much heavier, is much easier to work with. It should be packed in firmly about an inch thick all around the hub after the oakum, which is a tarred, ropelike substance, has been tamped in firmly.

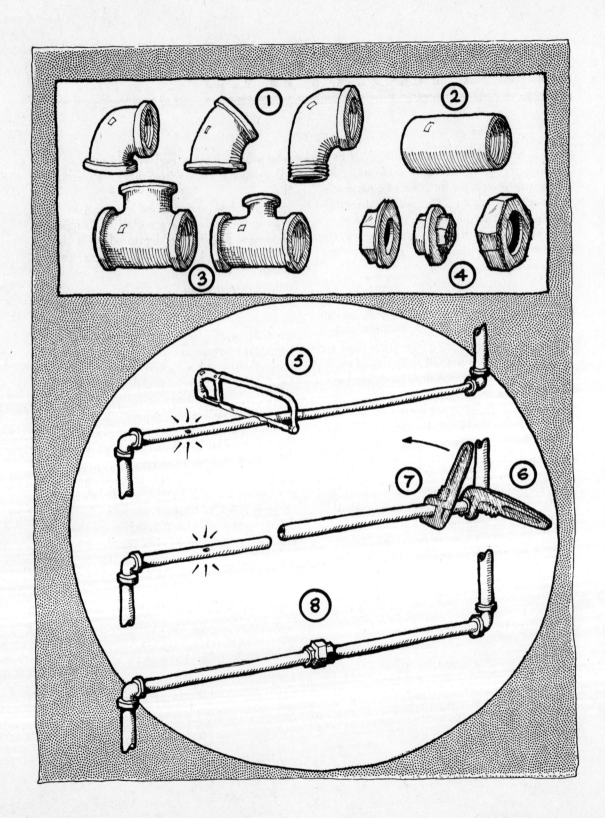

THREADED-STEEL PIPES

A lot of older plumbing that is not copper is made of lengths of galvanized steel pipe, threaded at the ends and held together by a variety of fittings such as elbows ①, couplings ②, tees ③, and unions ④.

Providing it is measured correctly, steel pipe is very easy to assemble. All you need is some joint compound to smear on the threads to make them watertight and two pipe wrenches to turn the pipes into the various fittings.

Should a pipe become too damaged to be repaired with a clamp (as on page 101), its replacement is very simple. Turn off the main water supply and drain the entire system by opening the lowest and highest faucets. Saw through the middle of the length that is damaged ⑤, using a hacksaw, and then remove both pieces.

Use two wrenches: one to hold the fitting immobile ⑥, and the other to unscrew the pipe ⑦—you do not want to unscrew the fitting! While doing this, take care not to let an overly long heavy length of unsupported pipe hang down freely—it could do damage to the rest of the system.

The next step is the most critical—but is by no means difficult. You must measure the distance between the two remaining fittings, and then, in order to provide enough pipe to be screwed *into* these fittings, add an amount equal to the inside diameter of the pipe. Thus, if the pipe you are working with has an inside diameter of ¾ inch, add ¾ inch for *each* fitting to the overall length.

You cannot replace the removed length with one piece of pipe because as you screwed in one end you would be unscrewing the other end! Therefore you must cut the new pipe into two pieces and screw in first one end and then the other, finally joining the two pieces with a fitting known as a union ④, which is designed specifically for this purpose. The insertion of the union also takes up space, so *one* of the pieces should be shortened, as before, by an amount equal to the inside diameter of the pipe being used. Note that although you might think that because the union receives pipe on both sides it should equal two fittings, you subtract only *one* diameter's length from the pipe.

If you have worked all these measurements out beforehand on paper it is a simple matter to buy the two required lengths precut and prethreaded from a plumbing house. It is very easy to thread pipe but the equipment is expensive, so have it done by a professional.

Make sure the threads on the pipes and in the fittings are clean, and coat them liberally with joint compound—you can buy large or small amounts in cans or tubes. Using two wrenches as before (one to hold the fitting and one to turn the pipe), thread the pipes firmly into the existing fittings.

Finally, install the union ⑧, which can be tightened without exerting any pressure on any other part of the system. If, after having turned the water back on, anything leaks a little, simply give the offending joint another half turn.

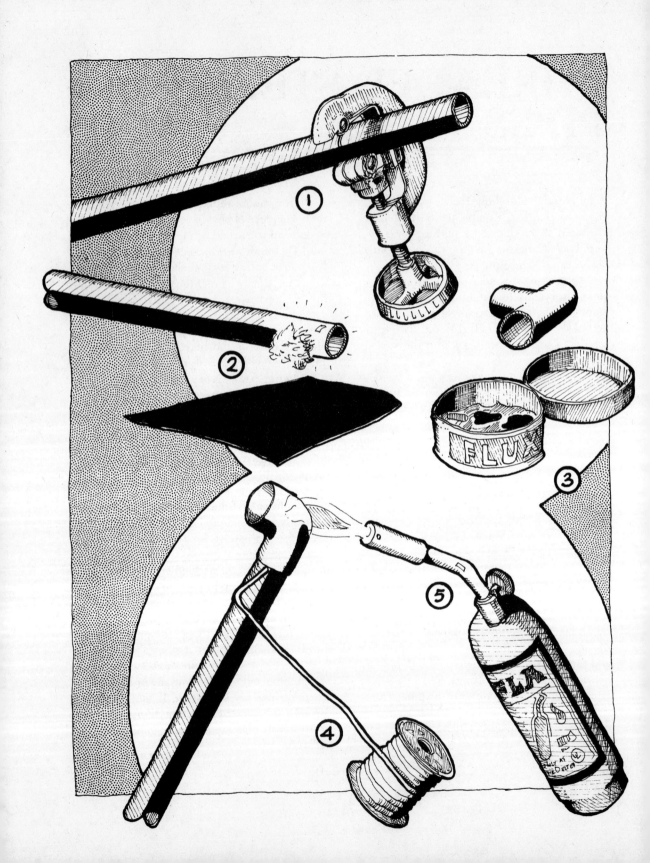

COPPER PIPE JOINT SWEATING

Although copper pipe is expensive, it is for several reasons the best. It does not accumulate sediment, it is corrosion resistant, it is stronger than plastic, and it is easy to install. Knowing how to join various lengths together—a process known as "sweating a joint"—is very useful since it will enable you to repair, replace, or even improve your system. You will never have to worry about a sudden leak or a burst pipe turning into an emergency that shuts the whole house down while you wait for the plumber to arrive.

If a joint is leaking, or if a section of pipe is damaged, you will, of course, turn off the water and drain the pipes. Then heat the nearest fittings with a butane torch ⑤ until they can be pulled apart. Measure any pipe to be replaced the same way as steel pipe is measured (see the previous section), but cut it with a special tubing cutter ① rather than a hacksaw. A hacksaw will work but leaves ragged edges to be filed. The pipe cutter does a much better job and is a relatively inexpensive tool.

The next step is the most important if you are to make a leakproof joint: clean the end of the copper pipe and the inside of the fitting with emery cloth or wire wool ② until both shine. Dirty pipe will not take solder and will undoubtedly leak.

Next, coat the end of the pipe with flux ③ and join all of the pieces together. You will need both hands for the next operation so if the pipe needs to be supported to hold it together do so now.

Solder comes in spools ④; unwrap 6 to 10 inches and bend the last inch over at right angles—this gives you the right amount for the joint and also makes it easier to get the solder around the back of the joint.

Now heat the fitting. Do not heat the pipe or the ends of the fitting—heat the thickest part of the fitting ⑤. This way the whole joint will become hot enough within a minute or so to accept the solder. When the joint is hot enough it will draw the solder into itself when you touch the joint with the end of the solder—even if the joint is upside down, because the process works by capillary action. Only a thin line of solder should remain visible around the joint. You should not use more than an inch of solder or the excess will build up inside and possibly cause a blockage.

A couple of useful tips to bear in mind: if you are sweating a joint which is so close to another joint that there is the danger that heat from the torch will also melt the second joint, wrap a damp rag around it; if you are sweating a fitting that takes more than one piece of pipe, fit all the pipes into the fitting at the same time and sweat everything together at once.

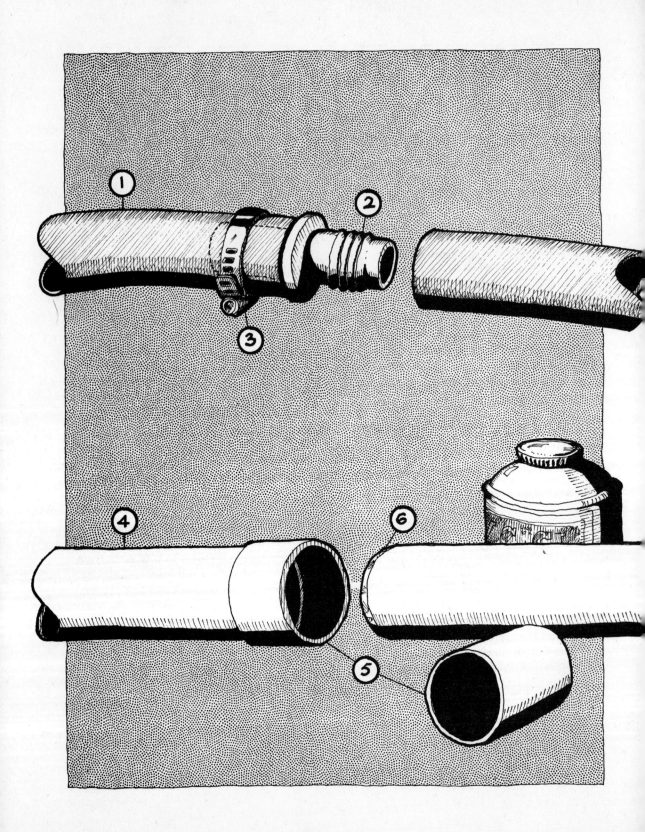

PLASTIC PIPE

Plastic pipe, which comes in various types commonly referred to by their initials, such as PVC, ABS, and CPVC (for the simple reason that their full names are rather a mouthful—PVC stands for polyvinyl chloride, for example), is not allowed everywhere. There are many local building codes which restrict the use of some if not all kinds of plastic pipe, so it is very important to check before you start replacing anything with plastic pipe.

Although not all of the above-mentioned types are equally good for all jobs—only CPVC is good for hot water, for example—they are all extremely easy to work with. PVC can be fitted together by hand, and at most, the rigid plastic types merely need a little gluing.

But first understand the limitations. ABS, for example, is the kind used for large waste lines. Although it is not subject to the corrosion which so often attacks metal pipes, it has nothing like the strength of cast iron, and so it is dangerous to bury it in situations where it might become crushed. Plastic pipe also has disadvantages if it's used for a cold water supply line. If you live in an area subject to freezing weather and need to insulate your pipes, you run the risk of melting the plastic if you use heat-tape and the water supply should stop! CPVC, although it is designed for use with hot water, can only handle temperatures up to 180 degrees F (82 degrees C). It is therefore important to make sure that the pressure relief valve on the hot water heater is set to work before this temperature is reached. Since plastic pipe does not have much compressive strength, it should be braced wherever it is to be subjected to any strain—such as in long unsupported overground runs.

PVC ① may be sold in long rolls (up to 100 feet) and only needs to be cut to length with a hacksaw. The rigid types are sold in standard shorter lengths but may be similarly cut with a hacksaw. Always take care to make a square cut across the pipe and clean the rough edges and any burrs with sandpaper.

To join lengths of PVC simply push the pipe onto the ridged fitting ②. For complete security install a stainless steel hose clamp ③. The fit is designed to be very tight so it helps to work with pipe that is warm rather than cold—but be very careful about heating it with a torch, because it melts quickly. Sometimes, rubbing a little soap on the fitting will help it all go together more easily.

Rigid plastic pipe ④ goes *inside* its fittings ⑤. Fitting is easier if you taper ⑥ the edge of the pipe a little with a sharp knife. If the pipe is shiny, a light rubbing with sandpaper, as well as ensuring that the pipe and the fitting are clean, will guarantee good adhesion. The glue should be brushed onto the end of the pipe and inside the fitting. Since the glue dries in a few seconds, always fit everything dry first to make sure that all the lengths are correct. When the glue has been applied, fit the pipe and fitting together with a twist and leave it for twelve hours before running any water through it.

One final precaution—anything that leaks should be cut out and replaced rather than patched; it is after all very easy to do.

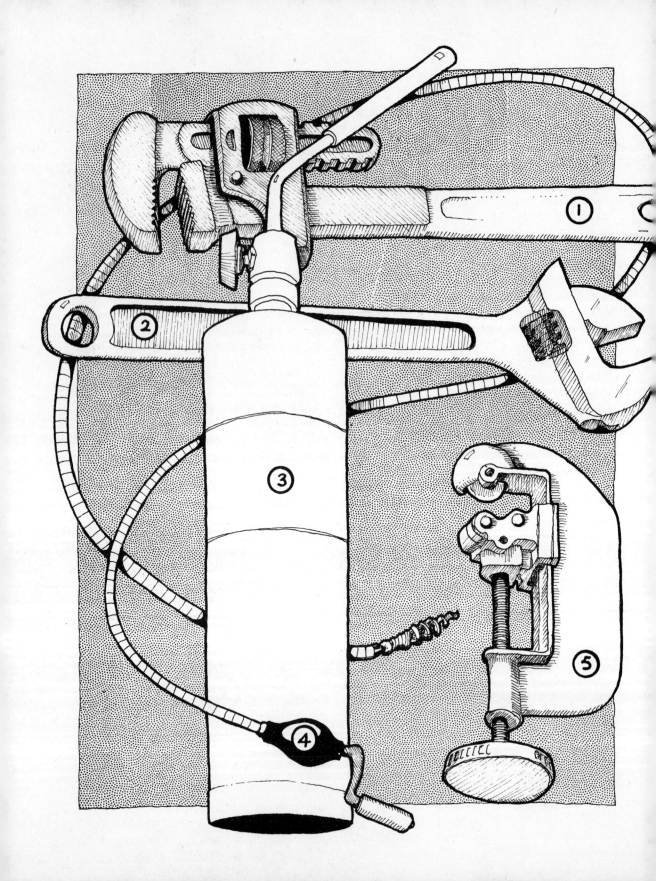

TOOLS

Probably the most useful tool when working with pipes and plumbing fixtures is the pipe wrench ①. Pipe wrenches are made in various sizes from small to very large indeed, but for most domestic jobs a 10-inch wrench is adequate. They are designed to be used in one direction only, and the outer jaw (the one that moves when the adjusting wheel is turned) is made so that when the wrench is pulled toward you it will grip round pipe in its teeth, but when it is pushed away from you the jaws will open up. Consequently, you do not need to screw the jaws down tightly onto the pipe you want to turn—loosely is sufficient. Your pulling action will be enough to hold the pipe fast.

It is not a good idea to use the pipe wrench on nuts, even large nuts, for it will surely round the edges of the nut until nothing can grip it anymore. For large nuts use an adjustable wrench, such as the crescent wrench ②. Like the pipe wrench, the crescent wrench should also be used only in one direction—if the one shown were around a nut you would only pull the handle to the top of the page. If you wanted to turn the nut the other way you would turn the wrench over first. This way you minimize the possibility of the wrench slipping off the nut—something which often results in painfully skinned knuckles when it happens. The crescent wrench should, however, be tightened down on the nut before any attempt is made to turn it.

A propane torch ③ is also indispensable if you are going to do any pipe fitting, and is also useful for heating nuts that have "frozen" fast. A little heat expands the metal and sometimes makes it easier to loosen a nut. A word of caution when using these torches: always make sure that the nozzle and valve stem are screwed on firmly to the actual bottle, or gas may leak and ignite.

The plumber's snake ④ and its companion, the plumber's friend, have been described on page 111. They have no substitutes; you may not need them often but when you do they are invaluable. Since they are so inexpensive no house should be without them.

The tubing cutter ⑤ also comes in a variety of sizes for cutting large or small pipe. For most household plumbing a cutter that can handle pipe with an outside diameter of up to 1½ inches is large enough. They are usually fitted with little sliding reamers for cleaning up the inside edges of the freshly cut pipe. Many people get along quite nicely without them, using instead a hacksaw with a medium-toothed blade.

Professional plumbers will have many more larger and complicated tools, most of which are quite expensive—such as a tap and die set for threading steel pipe—and which do not warrant being bought for one job. For this reason jobs demanding these tools are best left to outside help. With the usual complement of household hammers, screwdrivers, and the odd pair of pliers, however, you will need little else other than the tools described here to take care of most common household problems.

PART FOUR

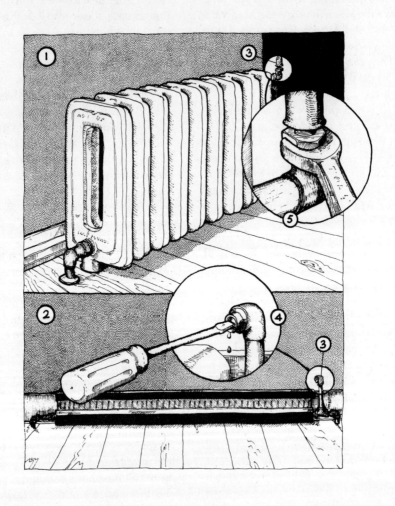

HEATING AND COOLING REPAIRS

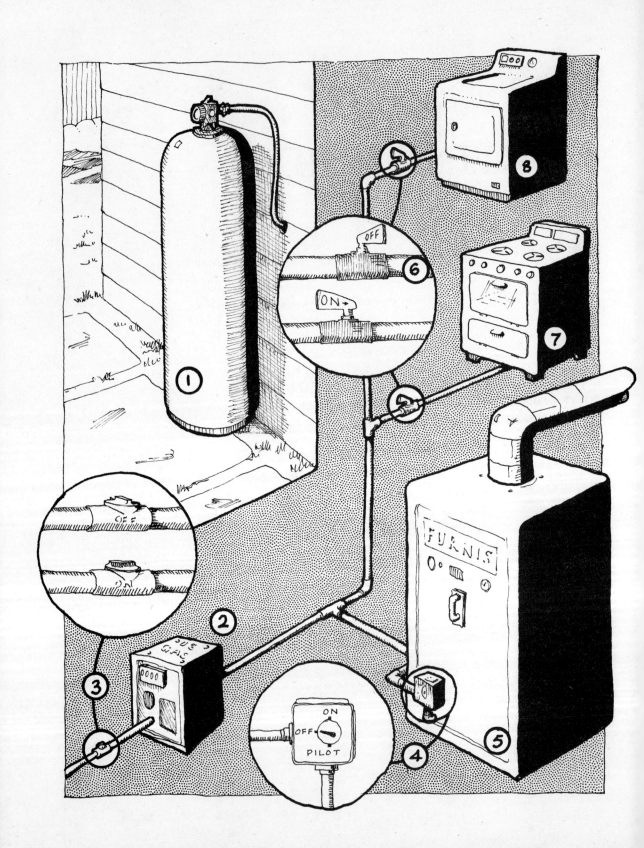

GAS!

Apart from an actual burning fire, the smell of gas should be treated as one of the most serious emergencies you can encounter in the home. Because the potential for catastrophic explosion is so great, the gas that is used in the home, which is naturally odorless, has an extra substance called mercaptan added to it. Mercaptan not only can be smelled easily in very small amounts but also has a distinct and memorable aroma. If you are not sure what it is, turn on the gas just a fraction so that a little escapes without igniting—one sniff will be enough for you to recognize it next time.

When you do smell gas, unless you can immediately pin the source down to a blown-out pilot light or something equally simple and curable, the rule is to turn off the supply—quickly! To be able to do this you need to understand where the gas comes from and where it goes. People who live in rural areas and many suburban areas often keep their own supply of gas in tall cylinders ① located just outside the house, or in larger tanks sometimes buried in the ground. These tanks have two valves, one for filling the tank with gas and the other for controlling the flow out. The latter valve is usually found in the thin copper tubing that conducts the gas from the tank to the house. The connections here are among the most common sources of leaks, and any smell emanating from this area should prompt a quick tightening of all nuts. If this does no good, turn off the main supply valve and call your supplier, who will normally respond very quickly.

City users get their gas from utility companies who pipe it in to the house through a meter ②, usually located outside the building. Just before the meter will be found the main shutoff valve ③, which commonly can be operated only by pliers or a wrench. It is a good idea to know exactly where this valve is and keep the proper tool handy to turn it on and off with.

Inside the house, the gas may run to one or more appliances. Sometimes only a cooking stove is supplied with gas, but in other cases the whole house is run on gas, using various pipes and branch lines. Individual appliances usually have their own controls which allow the supply to be shut off while leaving the pilot light still burning. Such a control ④ is typically found on furnaces ⑤ and hot water heaters.

In the line before each appliance you should also find a simple on-off valve ⑥ which controls the supply to that appliance only. These are usually marked, but if not, the commonest arrangement is that the supply is off when the handle is turned across the pipe, and on when it is in line with the pipe.

Go and find all these valves so that you know in advance how and where to turn everything off. Under no circumstances try to locate a leak with the aid of a burning match! Once you've shut off the supply, call for service; utility companies will come faster for suspected gas leaks than for anything else.

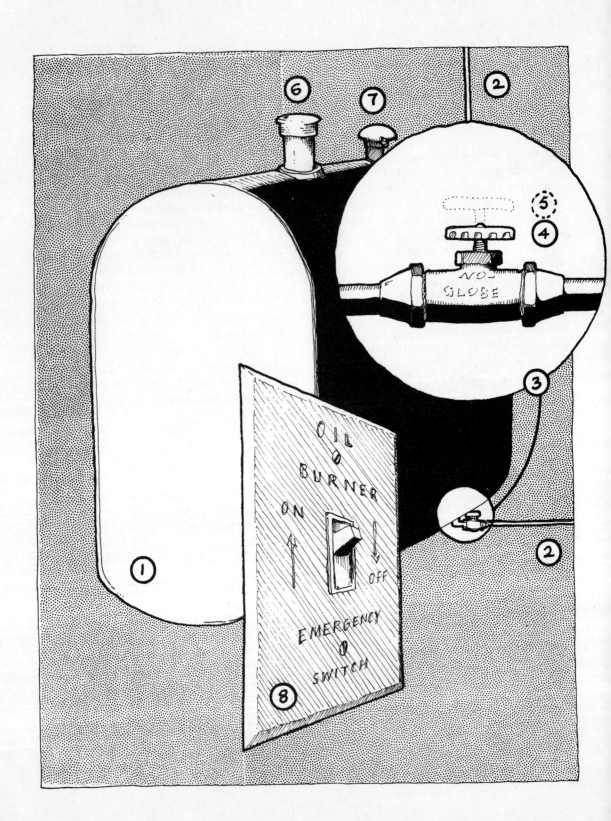

FUEL OIL SMELL

Oil-fired furnace problems are discussed more fully on page 141 but what is important here is what to do when you notice a strong smell of oil in the house. As with gas, the safest thing to do is to immediately turn off the supply, since a system in good operating order should not smell. A strong smell suggests trouble—and possibly dangerous trouble of an explosive and fiery kind.

Oil is stored in large tanks ① above or below ground outside the house, or in similar tanks inside, in the basement or cellar. If you have an outside tank and it is aboveground, it should not be hard to find. There will be one or two copper lines ② running from the tank to the house. These are the supply lines. Where they leave the tank, sometimes underneath and sometimes from on top, is the place to look for the first shutoff valve ③. These are designed differently than gas valves—they look very much like water valves, with round handles. When they are screwed all the way in ④ the oil may flow; when they are in the screwed-out position ⑤ the flow is cut off. Should a fire start in the line the inside of the valve is supposed to melt and pop out—thus automatically shutting down the supply.

If the tank is buried, all that is visible will be the oil filler tube ⑥, through which the tank is refilled, and a vent tube ⑦. In this case, and in many cases of aboveground tanks with topside takeoffs, there won't be a shutoff valve at the tank. You will have to go directly to the furnace itself to find the valve in the supply line, usually just before a filter unit.

However, if you have noticed a strong smell of oil, you may not want to crawl into the basement and get next to a potentially dangerous furnace in order to shut off the supply. The next best thing to do is to cut off the electricity. Without electricity the pump and the burner will not operate and no oil can ignite. You have several options for shutting off the electricity; they are as follows.

Most simply, you can pull the main power switch (see page 51). Or, with a little more time, you can locate the specific circuit that feeds the oil burner, and either pull the fuse or trip the breaker, as the case may be (see page 53).

Additionally, most furnaces have their own emergency switches ⑧. If you know where these are, this is the best thing to do. A good system will have one somewhere in the house, usually near the service box, and a second one by the furnace itself, especially if the furnace is in the basement or cellar (so that a serviceman can disconnect the power more conveniently when working on the furnace).

Not so safe, but immediately effective, is turning the thermostat all the way down. After having done this, make sure that you go and find the emergency switch. Finally, call for professional help. Do not switch the system back on until the cause of the smell has been determined.

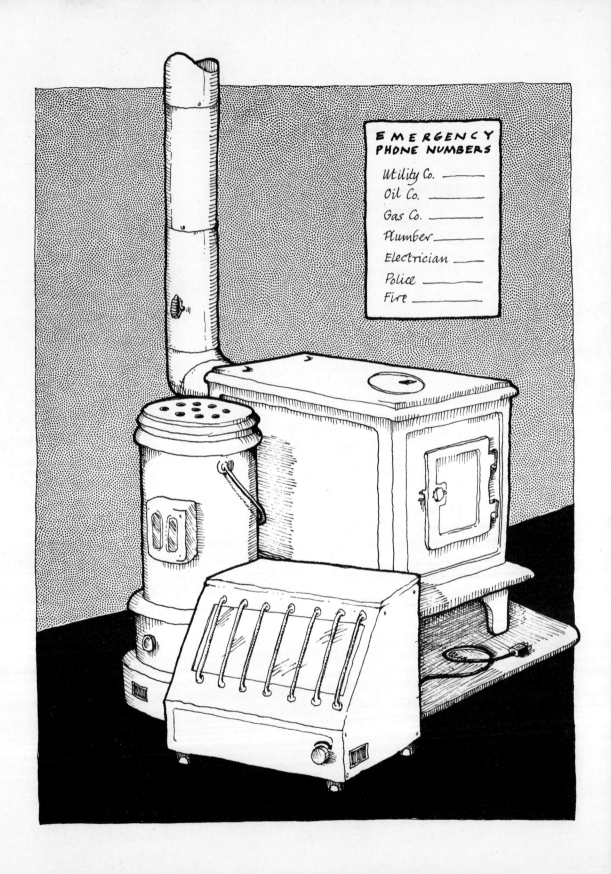

EMERGENCY
PHONE NUMBERS

Utility Co. _____
Oil Co. _____
Gas Co. _____
Plumber _____
Electrician _____
Police _____
Fire _____

NO HEAT!

For people who live in cold sections of the country, the sudden loss of heat in mid-winter can be an emergency bordering on crisis. It is not as bad for people in urban areas—who can call on landlords or seek refuge with neighbors—as it can be for people in rural areas with no one but themselves to rely on, but it is still a situation which invariably demands some immediate action.

The causes of heating-plant failure are varied, and range from natural disasters, such as trees knocking down power lines, to any one of a number of possible malfunctions occurring in your own system.

Aside from personal discomfort, which in extreme situations can, of course, be very serious, there are a number of other consequences to be aware of. Damage to houseplants, damage to any number of substances that deteriorate in below-freezing temperatures—such as paints, putties, and numerous household hardware supplies—and spoiling of foodstuffs are all things to be aware of, quite apart from the obvious risk to the plumbing if the pipes should freeze.

Therefore, when faced with a midwinter loss of heat, two courses of action should be pursued as simultaneously as possible: restoring the heat, and protecting all that is vulnerable.

So far as the first item goes, you should always have handy the relevant telephone numbers to call in an emergency: the power utility, in case of electric or gas supply failure outside the home (you should never rely on the next person notifying the company—there is always the possibility that you are the only one affected); the oil company or gas company that supplies you, and that services your furnace in the event of breakdowns; the local plumber and electrician; and if all else fails, at least the local police.

How serious the outage is and how long you are likely to be without heat, and how cold it is at the time, will determine what you do about the second item. Specific heating-system problems are discussed elsewhere, and it may be that something can be done immediately. In the event that you are going to have to rely on outside help, it is a very good idea to have available some source of backup heat.

Many houses, of course, have fireplaces, and these days wood stoves, as well. These are only useful in an emergency as long as you have fuel to burn and they are in operating condition. This means that a supply of wood or coal, and clean chimneys should be seen to at the beginning of each heating season.

For many people a portable kerosene heater is probably more convenient. This should be treated with a great deal of respect but can be invaluable in an emergency: if not for heating the whole house then at least for preventing damage to the plumbing.

If you have lost your heat but still have electricity, portable electric heaters are very useful. If there is nothing else to hand, a light bulb kept burning near a vulnerable water line can often prevent freezing.

The use of the kitchen gas stove for heating, however, is not recommended. This appliance is meant to be used only when closed, and has no provision for proper venting when used with the oven door open. Whatever you do will ultimately be the result of your preparedness—so plan ahead.

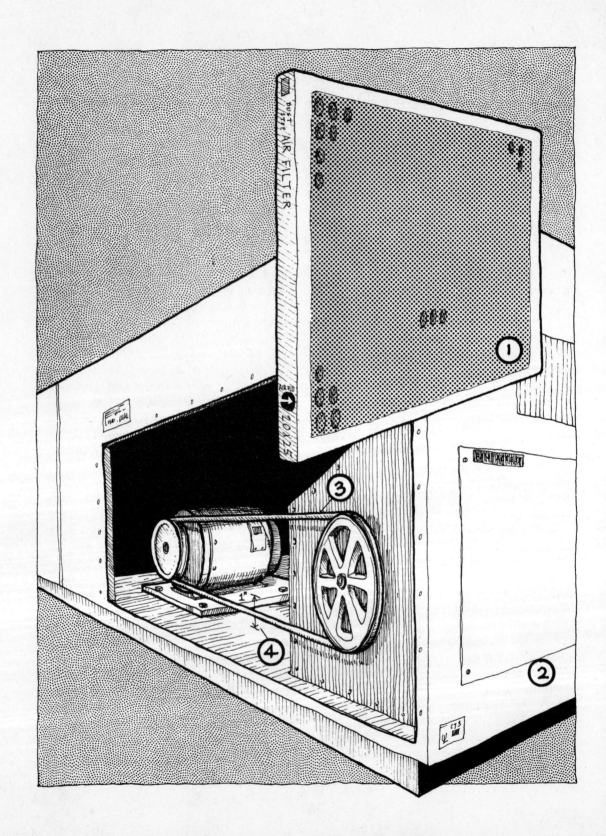

OIL-FIRED FURNACE PROBLEMS

Oil-fired furnaces are used to heat the air in hot-air heating systems or to heat the water in hot-water heating systems. The former systems incorporate a fan to force the hot air through a network of ducts to warm the house. The latter systems use radiators or baseboard units to carry the heated water around the house.

The following are some of the most common problems that can occur and what you can do about them before calling the repairman or serviceman.

The furnace will not ignite: Check that you are not out of oil, that the electricity is on, that the furnace emergency switch (see page 137) is on, that the fuse or circuit breaker controlling the furnace is intact or on, and check that the thermostat is turned up higher than room temperature.

The furnace ignites with a small explosion and an accompanying smell of oil: This is usually caused by incorrectly set electrodes within the burner and should be corrected at once by a professional repairman—too much oil is entering the combustion chamber before ignition occurs.

The furnace will not shut off: Turn the thermostat down. If this does nothing, the thermostat may be defective. The next thing to do is to shut off the emergency burner switch and call the repairman.

The furnace comes on more often than usual and for shorter periods of time: Check the filter ① (see also page 145)—if it is dirty and clogged this could be causing the trouble.

Otherwise you may have the thermostat in a bad location. If both the filter and the thermostat are all right then the problem is with the limit setting—this requires a serviceman.

The furnace ignites but no warm air comes into the room (with forced hot air systems): Assuming the registers and vents are not obstructed this indicates a problem with the fan ②—check first to see if the fanbelt ③ is broken. If it is, turn everything off and replace it. It may take some time to go and find the correct replacement but installation is no more difficult than replacing the fanbelt on an automobile. If the fanbelt is not broken it may just need adjusting. On some furnaces the fanbelt adjustment is very easy and obvious, but on others you may have to call for help. Remember that too loose a belt will slip and result in slow fan speeds with a consequent lessening of the amount of warm air that is sent through the ducts, but that too tight a belt can overload the motor. You should be able to deflect the belt not much more or less than an inch up and down ④. The fan pulley and the blower motor pulley should be lined up—problems can sometimes be caused by either one working out of alignment.

The fan won't stop: Some furnace fans have a manual switch which can be used to circulate air through the house when the furnace is not on—check that this manual switch is not on and that the filter is not clogged. Otherwise, the fan switch may be defective or there may be a short in the system, both of which possibilities require service.

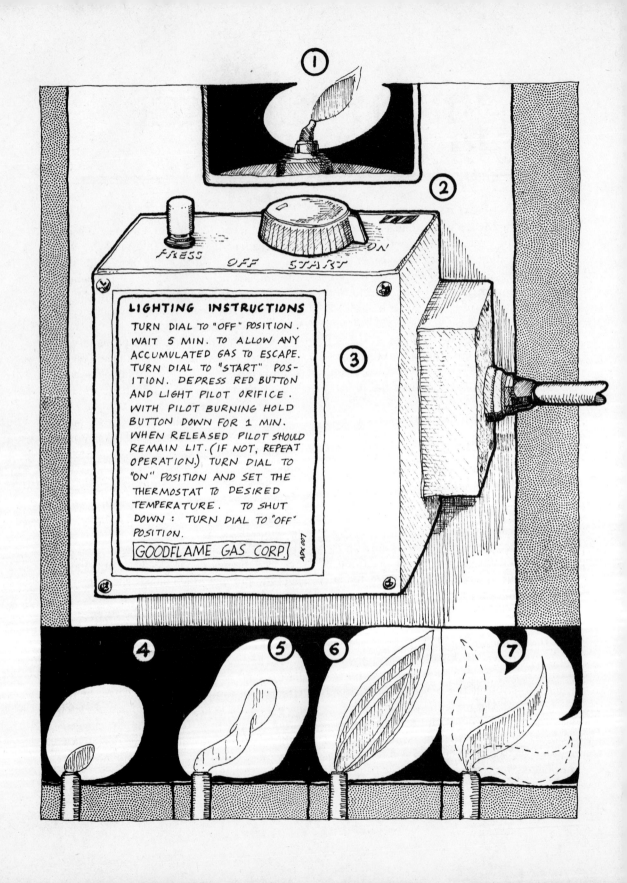

GAS-FIRED FURNACE PROBLEMS

In common with oil-fired furnaces, gas-fired furnaces sometimes have fans and blower motors, and the associated problems (see the previous section). But whether your gas heater is a direct heating unit—that heats through a floor register, or through a wall unit—or whether it heats forced hot air that is then ducted around the house and out of floor or wall registers, the most likely problems that you will encounter will be with the pilot light ①.

The first and most important rule is: if you should smell gas, turn off the main valve, extinguish all flames and cigarettes, open all the doors and windows, and call the serviceman or the utility company. This is very important because a gas smell could indicate a serious leak which could lead to a violent explosion.

Having said that, however, it must now be said that the most common problem is that the pilot light goes out. If the cause is that the pilot light control ② is in the off position, or a draft has blown it out, or that the pilot light orifice is dirty, you can rectify the situation yourself. Anything else requires the assistance of a qualified serviceman, for it may be that complicated things like the thermocouple or thermopile have gone bad, or that the heat exchanger is cracked or burned through.

If the pilot light is out, you can attempt to relight it by carefully following the instructions ③ that should be in evidence nearby (usually printed on an affixed plate). These instructions vary somewhat from manufacturer to manufacturer, but the following precautions invariably apply: turn off the gas to the main burner and the pilot and wait five minutes for any previously accumulated gas to disperse; turn the thermostat down below room temperature; and make sure that the filter and all registers are clean and unobstructed. If, after following the directions exactly, nothing happens, call for help, for something serious may be amiss.

If the pilot light does relight, check to see that it is burning correctly—a strong (but not violent) blue flame, with just a tip of yellow. To burn this way it must have just the right combination of air and gas; dirt and maladjustment can produce a defective flame which in turn can lead to a poorly operating furnace.

Listed below are some of the symptoms and causes of poor flames:

A small blue flame ④: Either the gas orifice is dirty or the gas pressure is too low—which could mean that your supply is low, especially if you use bottled gas.

A very yellow, weak flame ⑤: Insufficient air caused by an incorrectly set primary-air control, or dirt clogging the various ports, vents, and burner.

A noisy, violent flame ⑥: Too much air caused by an incorrectly set primary-air control, or dirt in the gas orifices.

A waving flame ⑦: Insufficient draft protection—either the cover for the pilot light is missing or some external cause needs to be shielded.

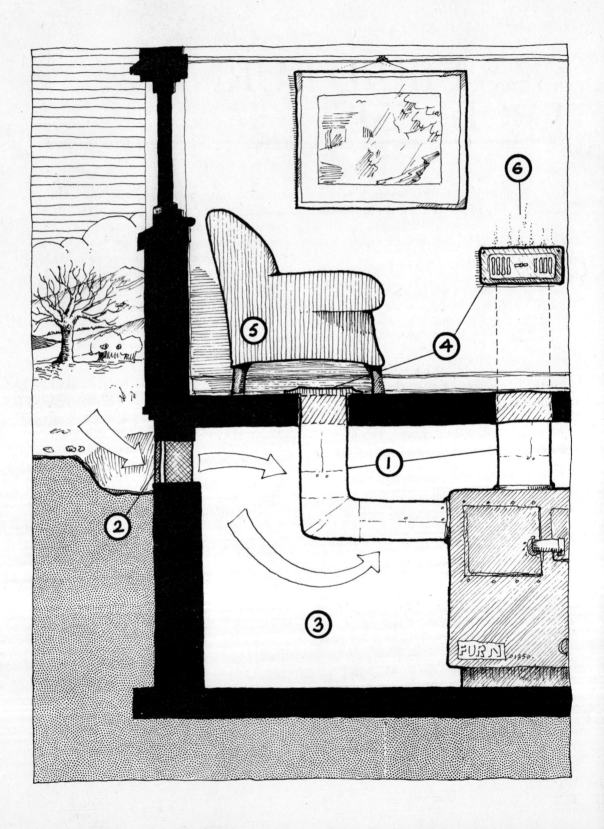

HEAT LOSS

Although your furnace (gas or oil) may appear to be working well, you may suddenly experience a significant heat loss and be at a loss to explain it. The answer may be connected with the ducts and vents that distribute the heat around the house.

Much heat can be lost when the metal ducts ① that carry hot air are routed through unheated and cold areas such as basements and crawl spaces. A sudden diminution in the amount of heat that appears to be coming up out of the floor registers could mean that an outside vent ② or opening into the basement has opened, allowing much colder air ③ to flow over the ducts. Check the outside perimeter of the house and make sure that everything is closed. Furthermore, much heat loss can be saved by insulating the ducts with a wrapping of fiberglass or an asbestos sleeve insulation. Even more efficient is the use of fiberglass ducts instead of metal ducts—and they are also quieter. Of course, any insulation that can be applied to the outside walls of the basement or crawl space will also cut down on heat loss from the ducts.

The other major problem that can contribute to heat loss is dirt. Starting at the furnace itself, the cold-air return filters must be kept clean, which means that they should be replaced regularly. A way to check whether they are still useful or not is to hold them up to the light and see if any light passes through. If they are completely clogged, replace them.

(Only furnaces with forced-air systems use filters, and the commonest type is the disposable kind illustrated on page 141 ①.) How often they need to be changed varies from situation to situation, but to be safe make an inspection at least twice during each heating season.

The next thing to check are the places where the heat actually enters the room. Forced-air systems are indicated by the presence of various floor or wall registers ④ in every room, while gravity systems usually heat through one large floor grill. Wall heaters, of course, are usually free standing, although they are sometimes partly hidden by being located in a closet. If you have this kind do not use the closet for storage: besides creating a fire hazard you could be inhibiting combustion and reducing the efficiency of the heater. That floor and wall registers should not be blocked by furniture ⑤ or covered by carpets is common sense, but this can sometimes happen accidentally, especially if you have pets or children.

Another warning sign that your system is dirty is the formation of streaky marks ⑥ around the registers. Make sure that the filters are clean and (turning the system off first) check the fan blades on the blower, cleaning them if necessary with a vacuum cleaner. A blower that is operating too fast may also cause dirty marks around the register. You should have a professional serviceman adjust this.

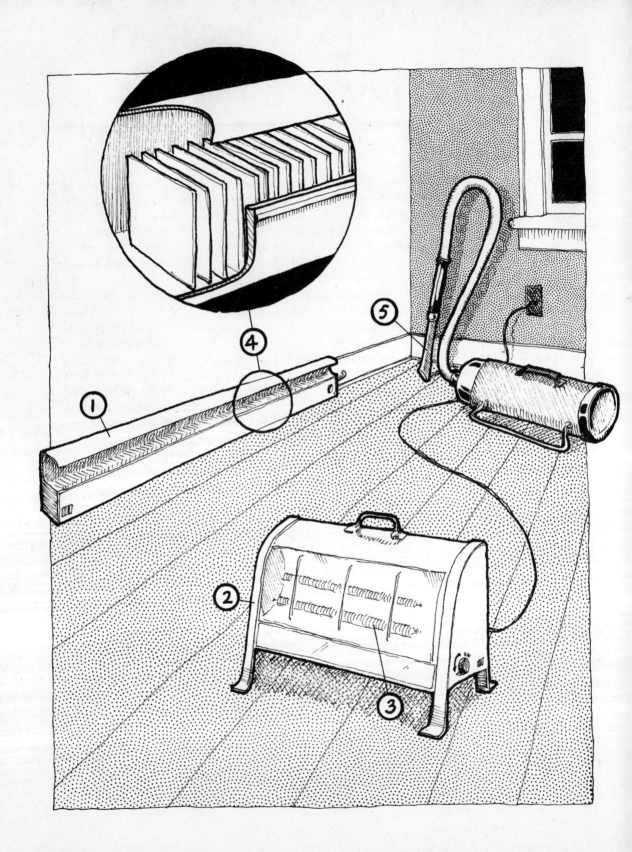

ELECTRIC HEATERS

There are two types of electric heaters in common residential use: baseboard units ① that are permanent fixtures, and portable electric heaters ② that may be plugged in wherever the need arises.

Since there are no moving parts on electric heaters (apart from various control knobs and thermostats), there is very little that can go wrong mechanically. The two chief causes of breakdowns and malfunctions are dirt and the wearing of wiring and elements. However, if an electric baseboard unit should fail to shut off (or fail to go on) it could constitute a real emergency.

Practically all electric heaters are now fitted with thermostats that automatically turn the heaters off when a certain temperature is reached. If this thermostat fails and the heater continues to work, all you have to do is to cut off its electricity supply. If the thermostat cannot be turned off, try unplugging the unit. If the unit is wired directly into the house's wiring, go back to the service box and pull out the fuse, or switch off the circuit breaker, that controls the circuit to which the heater is connected. If you can't immediately find this and are unsure which circuit is which, turn off the main switch (see page 51). Then, take your time to figure out which circuit is which so that you can eventually disconnect the heater

and turn everything else back on. Whatever you do, do not attempt to disconnect any wires leading into the heater; you might get a shock or create a fire hazard when you reconnect the electricity.

Before calling in an electrician, take a careful look at the unit and all visible wiring to see if anything is obviously disconnected or any wires are frayed, bare, touching, or broken. Repair of anything obvious like this could do the trick. It is generally easier to repair portable units than it is to repair baseboard units, since the portable heaters are easier to disassemble, and should it prove that the heating element ③ is worn or broken, it is a relatively simple matter to take it out and buy a replacement at any big hardware store or electrical supply house.

Dirt is the other main culprit. Baseboard units disseminate their heat via thin plates called fins ④, all lined up next to one another, usually under an outer cover. These fins are very susceptible to collecting dust and fluff, and becoming rapidly clogged. If a unit is then turned on after a period of disuse, a horrible smell may occur as the accumulated dust burns off. It is best to prevent this from happening by the simple expedient of a regular cleaning, using a thin vacuum cleaner attachment ⑤.

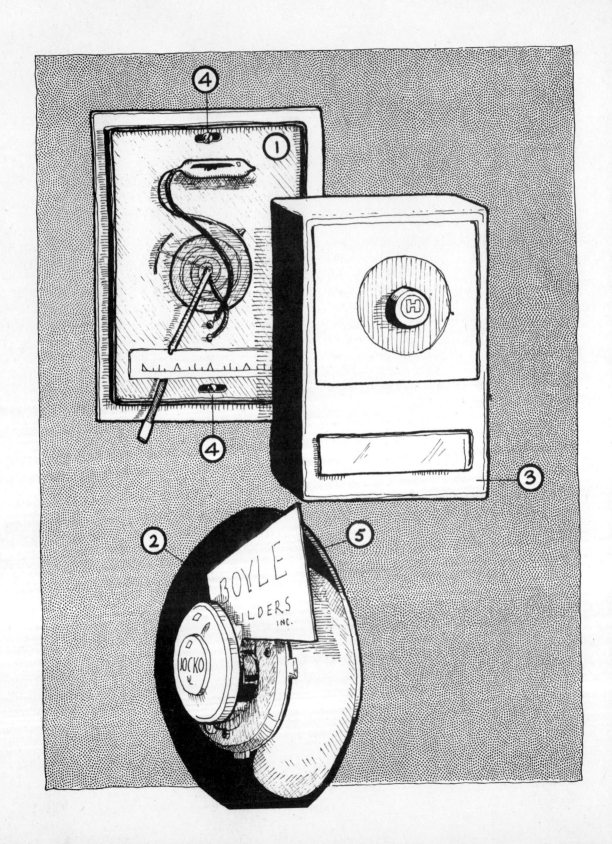

THERMOSTAT TROUBLE

Although thermostats are precision instruments they usually give years of trouble-free service. They require no servicing, no oiling, and provided they are adjusted correctly in the beginning, all that ever need to be done is an occasional cleaning.

Ignoring this need for cleaning can lead to one of two possible emergencies: one day you discover to your consternation that no matter how high you set the thermostat and no matter how low the room temperature falls you cannot get the heat to come on; or the opposite—even with the thermostat turned completely to the "off" position, the heat will not stop.

There are two basic types of thermostats commonly used to control domestic heating. One type operates with a little glass tube filled with mercury ①, and the other type ② depends upon a bimetallic strip—which is actually two strips of metal that separate or come together as the temperature changes, thereby switching the heat on or off.

Whatever your problem, first remove the face plate ③ or front cover from the thermostat to discover which type you have. Most thermostat covers simply pull off, but look carefully first for any retaining screws before you start pulling.

If the thermostat is of the mercury tube type it will only function if it is perfectly level.

Having been knocked into could have altered this, so you should check it with a carpenter's level, and readjust it if necessary. The adjustment is usually achieved by loosening one or two screws ④, and moving the whole thermostat.

If no mercury tube is apparent then you have the metal contact type ②. This is the kind that is susceptible to dirt. Unless the contact points are perfectly clean, the thermostat cannot function as a switch. Clean them as follows: turn the thermostat down—all the way. This will cause the contact points to open, and you can now, very carefully, slip in a thin piece of stiff paper, such as a business card ⑤. Now turn the thermostat all the way up, and the contact points will close—onto the card. Pull the card back and forth a few times to clean the points. Do not use any kind of sandpaper or emery cloth, for these are too abrasive; all that will happen is that you will scratch the points and achieve the same effect as if they were dirty.

An alternative method is to clean the points (and everything else that you can see with the cover removed), by gently using a very soft brush.

If, after all this cleaning and adjustment the thermostat still does not work correctly, then it is probably easier to have it replaced.

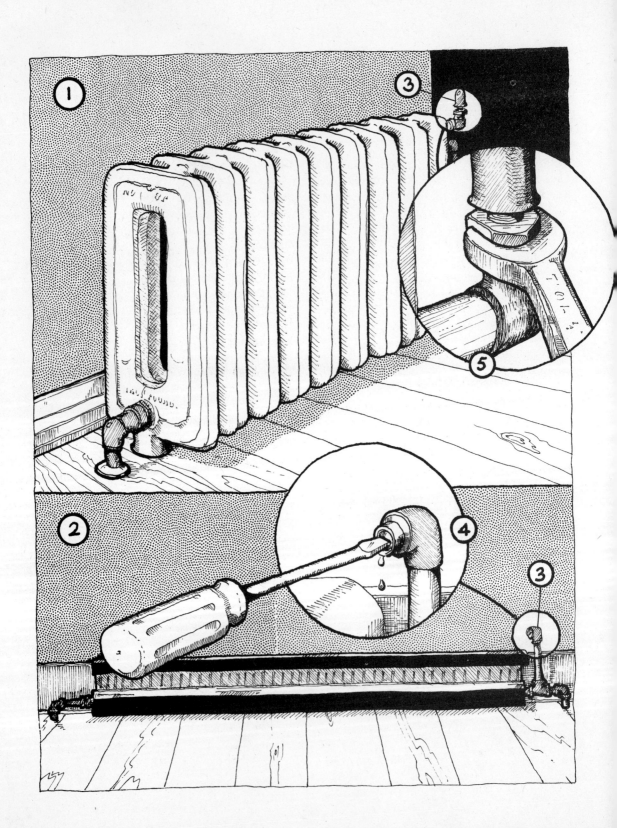

COLD RADIATORS

Radiators are used to heat houses either by steam or water. Steam is carried by the older, upright sort of radiator ① that is nice to sit on but not always so pleasant to look at. Hot water runs through the more modern baseboard units ② that look very similar to electric baseboard heating units.

The sheer size and weight of the upright kind is enough to "radiate" the heat successfully, but the baseboard units require the help of lots of parallel fins, arranged around the hot water pipes, to provide sufficient surface area to "radiate" effectively.

Despite these apparently significant differences, all radiators share two problems in common: they sometimes need to be bled, and they frequently need to be cleaned. Otherwise you will end up with cold radiators, even though the actual heating plant may be working well.

Both sorts have air vents ③ near the top which should be bled periodically to release trapped air—so that more water or steam, as the case may be, can flow through the radiator. Begin with the highest radiator in the house, or the one furthest from the furnace, and open the vent for a moment until water flows out

④. Then close it immediately—you do not want to lose more water than is necessary since it often contains expensive antifreeze. When the water flows out you know that all the air has been bled out.

Steam-radiator vent valves are designed to allow trapped air to escape automatically, and indeed, some are meant to allow the air to escape at different rates from radiator to radiator, thereby controlling the amount of heat given out by various radiators (to accomodate different needs), but these sometimes become clogged, and must be boiled out. This job, and its alternative—replacing the faulty vent valve—may not be something you want to do, but it is very easy to take a wrench and give a turn to the nuts at the base of the valve should the valve be leaking a little ⑤.

The other reason why radiators can become colder than previously is that they become clogged up with dust and lint. Their very design makes this a recurrent problem, and the only solution is regular cleaning, which is done most easily with a thin vacuum cleaner attachment. Not only the fins, but all other openings in the various radiator covers and grilles should be cleaned.

WOOD STOVE PROBLEMS

Wood stoves, which were once this nation's primary domestic "heating plant" but which then faded into rural obscurity, are once again becoming very common. The new generation of stoves, however, includes some radical departures from the old American potbelly stove ①. These changes, together with unfamiliarity with their habits, can lead to situations which can be quite worrying, and sometimes rate as full-blown emergencies.

The two basic problems which you may encounter are either not being able to get the stove to burn hot enough—or even burn at all—or suddenly realizing that the stove is burning far too hot.

There are few things more terrifying than the sudden discovery that the wood stove has turned cherry red and threatens to imitate a nuclear meltdown. This situation is invariably caused by having left the damper ② or draft controls ③ wide open. The first thing to do is to immediately close them down ④—but use caution, because undoubtedly they will be very hot to the touch. This will cut off the air supply and rapidly cut down the combustion rate, causing the fire to cool down, and probably, especially if the stove is a modern airtight model ⑤, causing it ultimately to go right out.

Do not (unless fire has already broken out and is consuming the house) pour water on the fire or the stove. This will possibly cause it to crack. If this happens, not only will you have ruined your stove, but you may end up with the fire all over the floor.

The stove should, of course, have been installed a safe distance away from all walls and other combustibles—such as curtains and carpets—but if you think the stove is getting too hot for safety, remove anything from the immediate vicinity that could possibly catch fire. If you feel you really have to dampen the fire, use sand or salt. Do not, in any event, take any chances; if there is the least doubt about the safety of the situation, call the fire department.

Being unable to get the fire to burn at all, on the other hand, is largely a matter of inexperience. Apart from mistakes such as leaving the damper closed and trying to ignite wet or damp wood, successful fire-lighting comes with practice and learning exactly how much paper and kindling to use, and which wood burns better to start with. But once again, a warning: do not, no matter how difficult lighting the fire seems to be, use anything like gasoline, kerosene, charcoal starter, or any similar liquid.

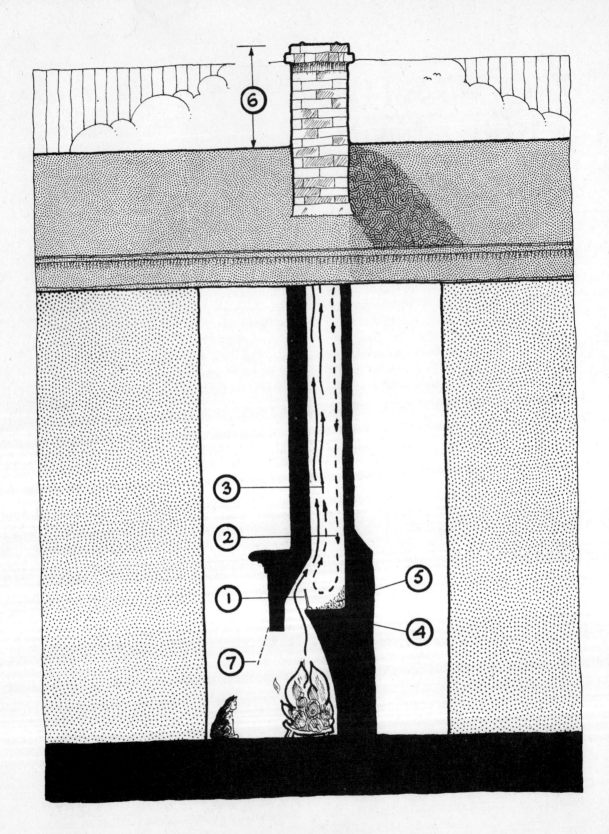

SMOKY FIREPLACE

Most fireplaces send puffs of smoke into the room on occasion—it is almost the nature of the beast—but a fireplace that is a chronic smoker is asking for some remedial attention.

If your fireplace has a damper ①, make sure it is open. The damper not only allows smoke upwards when it is properly opened, but also helps turn around the cold air that comes down the chimney ② and send it back up again, pulling with it the warmed air ③ from the fire.

Something which should be checked *before* the fire is lit is the cleanliness of the chimney and especially the smoke shelf ④. A properly constructed chimney will have a flat area just above the firebox which is designed to direct the downdraft back up the flue. In time, this shelf accumulates a lot of soot ⑤ to the point where the shelf becomes not only ineffective but dangerous—the soot can ignite and start a chimney fire.

That the top of the chimney should be unobstructed should be obvious, but overhanging branches or birds' nests sometimes accumulate, especially if the chimney has not been used for a while. Ideally this should have been checked when the chimney underwent its regular cleaning. What is not always so obvious, however, is that the chimney just may not be tall enough. (This may not be the fault of the original builder.) For the chimney to draw properly and not be subject to smoke-producing downdrafts, it must be higher than its immediate surroundings by at least 2 feet ⑥. This includes not only the roof through which it is built but also adjacent walls, roofs, nearby buildings, and even trees. If you cannot remove the obstruction you must increase the height of your chimney.

All of the above assumes that the fireplace itself, properly called the firebox, has been constructed on sound principles. This may not necessarily be so. There are a great many inefficient and wrongly built fireplaces, since the principles governing correct fireplace construction are not commonly well understood. Furthermore, location can play a big part in how well a fireplace works. The presence of a nearby hill, the situation of a house built under the eaves of a dense forest, or exposure on a high and windy heath can all affect how a fireplace works.

This is not the place for a discussion of rival firebox theories, but the following suggestions may be made for chronically smoking fireplaces. The easiest possible remedy is to install a hood ⑦ over the top of the fireplace. Whether this will work or not can be tested by holding a board across the top of the fireplace and gradually lowering it, observing closely whether or not the smoke stops coming out into the room. If it does stop, it might be possible to achieve the same effect by having a mason build up the hearth instead of installing a hood, or lowering the arch. Talk to several masons and discuss the possibility of altering the inside of the firebox. Perhaps a smoke shelf can be built if there is none; perhaps the sides or the back of the firebox can be flared more; perhaps the firebox can be converted to a different interior design, such as the extremely successful but radically different-looking Count Rumford–style fireplace, which is much shallower and taller than traditional fireplaces, but which works so well that its inventor, an American contemporary of Benjamin Franklin, was one of the most sought-after fireplace designers of his time.

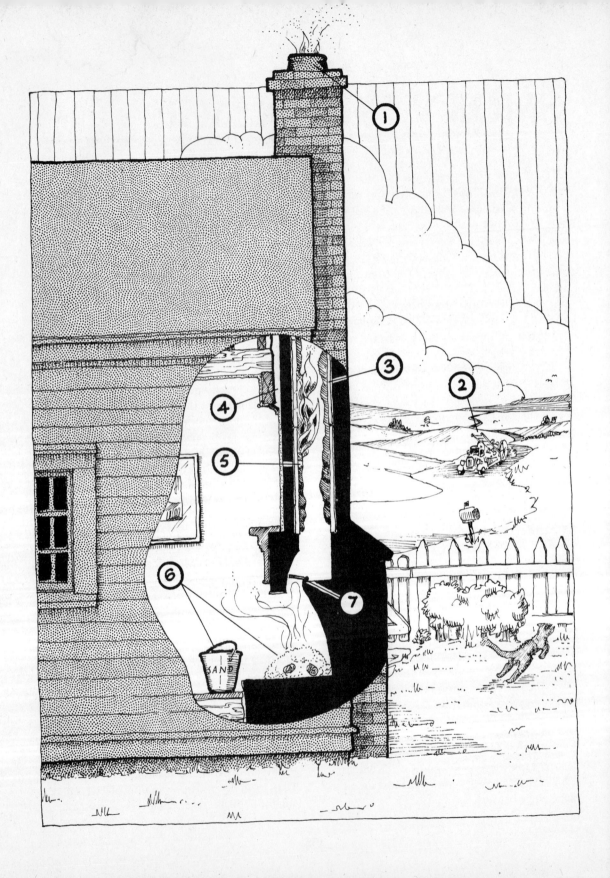

CHIMNEY FIRE

A chimney fire is the closest thing to actually having the house burn down—which is surely the ultimate household emergency—and can, unfortunately, sometimes progress that far. It is, therefore, one of the most serious occurences you are likely to have to deal with.

Even if you have never experienced a chimney fire before, it is unmistakable when it happens. The fire burns faster in the hearth or woodstove, and is accompanied by a terrifying roar from the chimney, much like the noise of a jet plane right in the house. As you rush outside, you observe sparks and soot ① shooting from the chimney.

Your first action should be to call the fire department ② not because they might be able to put the fire out any faster or more efficiently than you, but because if, in the tragic event that the fire in the chimney were to crack the flue lining ③, and ignite part of the house itself, they would be better equipped to save the whole house.

Cracking of the flue lining is, in fact, the chief danger. Providing that the integrity of the flue lining is maintained and that the chimney is built according to sound construction techniques—with adequate insulation between the masonry and any wooden framing in the house ④—nothing much can happen—apart from the burning up in the chimney of the combustible material that caused the fire in the first place. This material is the creosote ⑤ that has condensed on the inside of the flue, and which has gradually built up in thickness until the fire was burning hotly enough to ignite it.

Ideally, you should burn such fuel, and in such a way, that creosote is not formed, since it is not necessary and constitutes a potential hazard. It is the result of burning wood that is insufficiently seasoned, or that is too resinous (such as softwoods like pine); and of burning a fire too slowly—which means not hot enough to cause complete combustion. The various tars and gases rise up the chimney and condense on the cooler flue to form creosote.

Creosote is more apt to form in metal stovepipe than in masonry chimneys since the temperature difference inside and outside the stovepipe is greater than that of a masonry chimney, which by its sheer bulk provides a greater degree of insulation. A fire in a stovepipe can be most dangerous at the point where the stovepipe passes through the wall or the roof.

But to return to the chief danger—the cracking of the flue lining: If the fire is hot enough this may happen anyway, but it is almost certain to occur if you throw water on the fire and thereby change the temperature in the stack all at once. The way to put the fire out (in the grate, at least) is to douse it with sand ⑥ or bulk salt. Then close the damper ⑦ or draft controls. Since the fire cannot burn without oxygen you want to do everything you can to limit the supply.

Having done this, and while waiting for the fire department to arrive, keep an eye open outside for anything that might catch fire from the sparks being shot out of the chimney.

Prevention, in the form of a chimney sweep, is, of course, the best cure.

AIR CONDITIONER DIFFICULTIES

Although many people consider air conditioning to be a luxury (and indeed some consider it a nuisance), for many others it is a necessity, and a breakdown or malfunction can be a true emergency. Many problems will call for professional help, but do not assume that there is never anything you can do yourself.

If absolutely nothing happens when you turn the unit on, whether it be central air conditioning or a window unit, the first thing to suspect is a lack of power. Make sure that the window unit is indeed plugged in ①, and that no fuses are blown or circuit breakers tripped, and that there is power to the house. Central air conditioning systems often have reset buttons on the drive units, usually clearly marked as such, and all that needs to be done (after having made sure that the power is on) is to hold these buttons down for a few seconds to restart the system.

The next most common problem is that the unit runs but it doesn't seem to be cooling! Once again, don't jump to conclusions. First, check the thermostat setting ②. It could be that someone has turned it down. If the thermostat *is* set all the way to the coolest setting, however, check the filter. A dirty filter can effectively prevent an air conditioner from cooling. Filters in window units are usually found behind the front panel ③, which might

have to be unscrewed. Some are replaceable, some are designed to be cleaned and then sprayed with a dust-trapping coating. Central air conditioning filters are of the replaceable type, and in normal use should be changed twice a year.

The third possibility, a refrigerant leak, calls for a serviceman. The clue that this is the trouble is the appearance of an oily-looking deposit around the tubing or on the floor ④.

If the unit appears to be running slowly, it may be the result of low voltage. The way to check this is to turn on the room lights and then observe whether or not they dim appreciably when you turn on the air conditioner. If they do, you should either call the power company—there may be a brownout in progress—or arrange to have the air conditioner put on a separate electric circuit.

If you begin to hear unusual noises, something has either worked loose or become worn. If tightening all visible screws and mountings does not help, and you have checked that the noise is not caused by the case vibrating against itself, it may be that the fan bearings are worn and need to be replaced. Before ordering a new fan, check that the fan blades are not rubbing against their housing—you might be able to cure the problem by simply bending the fan blades a little.

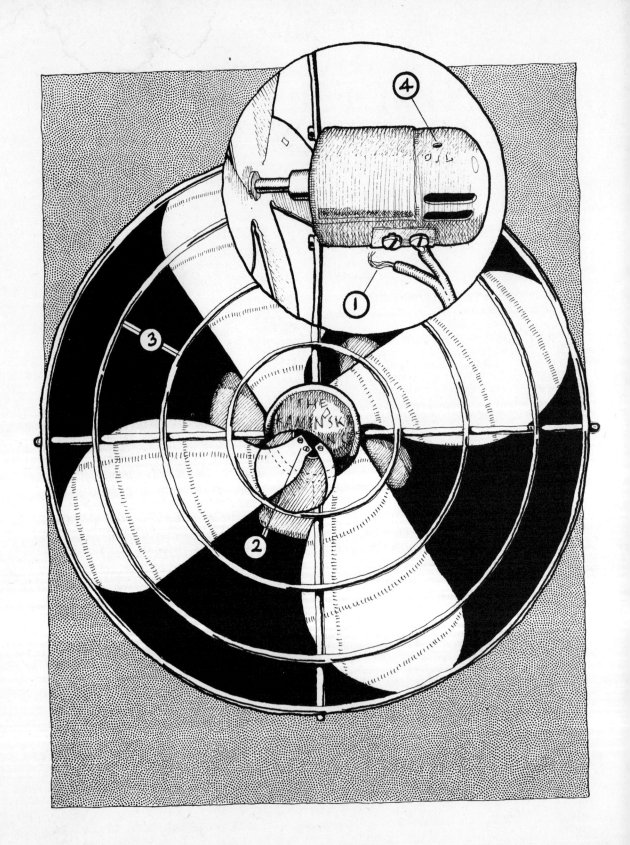

BAD FAN

There can be a surprising number of fans around a house, apart from the obvious—such as ceiling fans and desk fans. There are fans in range hoods, exhaust fans in bathrooms, fans in heating plants, and attic ventilating fans.

They are all designed to move air, usually hot, either in or out. Depending on their particular job their breakdown is typically evidenced by it suddenly becoming hotter or colder than you are used to.

Kitchen cookstove exhaust fans, usually found in range hoods but sometimes mounted in the wall near the stove, have (like heating plant fans, which are discussed at length elsewhere) filters which must be kept clean if the fan is to be effective. If the kitchen begins to smoke up—with the fan running—inspect the screen or filter in front of it. Sometimes this can be vacuumed clean, but more often it is best to remove it completely and wash the whole thing in warm soapy water.

Attic ventilating fans and bathroom fans are closely related—their job is to remove hot air to the outside. While bathroom fans are usually wired into the light switch so that they operate whenever the light is turned on (which is usually everytime the bathroom is used—it is the lack of a window that necessi-tates both light and forced ventilation), attic fans are generally wired to a thermostat, and go on only when the temperature in the attic reaches a certain upper limit. Wiring problems are common to both, and usually call for an electrician. It is worthwhile inspecting them before calling for help, but be sure the power is off before you start poking around.

A fan that does not run should be inspected for the following obvious faults: are there any loose, frayed, or disconnected wires ①, are the blades tightly attached to their hub ②, or are they loose and perhaps jammed against the casing? If only one blade is bent this can cause a noisy wobble—check the grill ③ around the fan frame.

Attic fans sometimes become obstructed by small would-be attic lodgers; bats or squirrels and the like can find their way into the housing and become stuck. For this reason you should check that the fan is fitted with a wire screen on the outside, and that this is inspected regularly to see if it is still whole.

Lastly, most fans require a drop of oil in the bearings ④ once in a while—without it they may squeak, run slowly, or, in severe cases, not run at all.

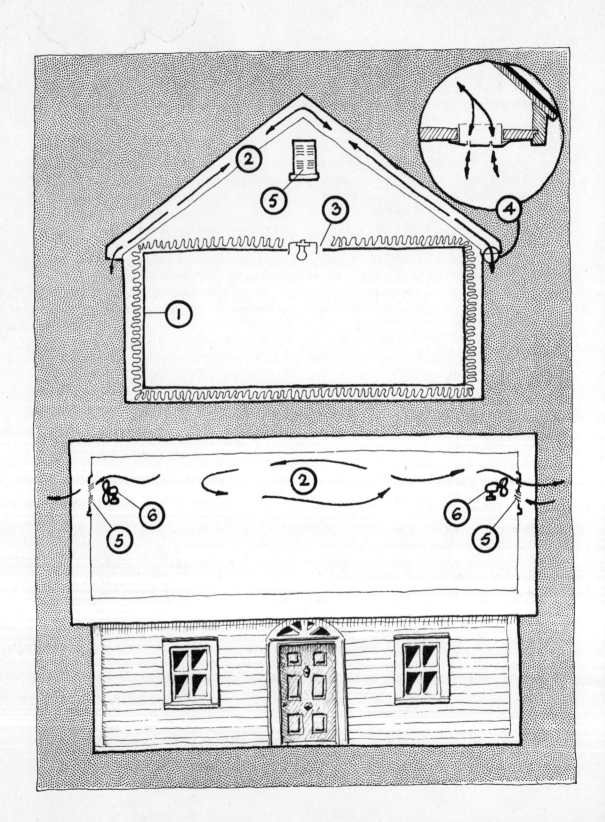

CONDENSATION DRIP

It sometimes happens that leaks occur in the ceiling when it is not raining, and yet the water is disconcertingly real. Apart from the possibility that the leak is from a defective water storage tank kept in the attic or from some overhead plumbing, it will usually be found to be the result of moisture already in the house having condensed against a cold surface, such as the inside of the roof.

This is a relatively modern malady rarely met with in older houses, since older houses invariably had attics and not much insulation. It can happen when an insulated house is heated in winter and when for various reasons the air in the house has a relatively high moisture content which is usually welcome because it is much more comfortable than dry air—and there is no vapor barrier, or at best a faulty one.

The warm moist air rises in the house and, unless the insulation is completely impermeable, finds its way to the uninsulated inside covering of the house. Since the outside is at a much lower temperature (in the winter), the water vapor condenses on the cold surface and runs down rafters and studs until it appears on the ceiling below as water stains or actual drips.

Providing the area immediately inside the outermost skin of the house is well ventilated, the condensation does not amount to much—in fact, it tends to evaporate almost immediately. Alternatively, if there is a perfect vapor barrier (of either continuous insulation or plastic sheeting) between the warm air inside the living space and the cold inside of the house's exterior skin, no condensation can occur because no moisture can reach the cold surfaces.

Should the condition occur, therefore, there are two things you should try to do: repair, or provide for, an effective vapor barrier ①; and establish some ventilation ② to carry away the moisture-laden air before it has a chance to condense and become a problem.

By following the procedures outlined on page 31 (for looking for roof leaks), you should be able to locate the source of the condensation. If this has led you to the attic, look first of all for gaps in the insulation ③ through which warm air from the heated part of the house may be escaping. Typical spots are around ceiling light fixtures, electrical wiring, and even plumbing pipes. Fill these gaps! It can be hard to tell if there is a vapor barrier (although condensation is an almost sure sign that there isn't), but in extreme cases you will have no alternative but to remove the interior finish and install one.

At the same time, do all you can to improve, or provide, adequate attic ventilation. Make sure there are vents in the eaves ④ and gables ⑤ sufficient to allow an effective air flow, helping it along if necessary with the aid of an attic ventilating fan ⑥, positioned to move the air through all parts of the roof.

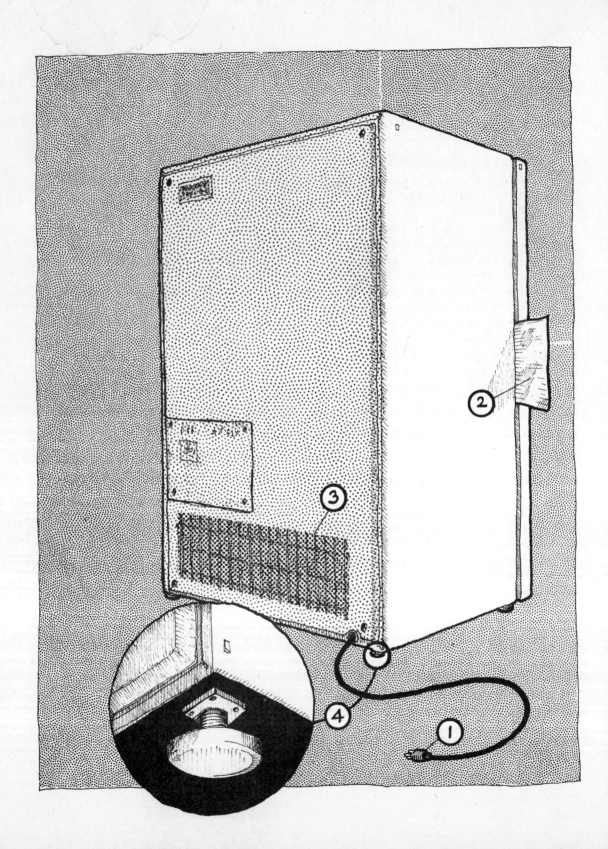

REFRIGERATOR PROBLEMS

At first glance there wouldn't appear to be much that one could do with a faulty refrigerator, yet there are a number of complaints (which can border on emergency status) that can be attended to quite easily by almost anyone.

Refrigerator does not run: These days most refrigerators are run by electricity—so check that the refrigerator is plugged in ①; check that the circuit breaker or fuse controlling it is in order (see page 53); and, of course, check that the power is on to the house (this may not be obvious—if it is in the middle of a warm day there may be no lights or heating appliances on to give you any indication of a power outage). Finally, check that the thermostat inside the refrigerator is on.

Refrigerator will not stop running: First check the thermostat—if it is set too low this could be the reason for continuous operation. Next, check that the door is shut properly. To check this, insert a piece of paper into the door ②. If, with the door shut, you can pull the paper out easily, then the door is not shutting properly.

There are two possible remedies for this: tightening or adjusting the door hinges if possible, or replacing the seal—which does eventually lose its resiliency and may need to be replaced. On some models replacement is very easy but on most you will need professional help. A third possible cause is excessive dirt on the grills and coils usually found on the back of the refrigerator ③. This area often escapes cleaning, and consequently all kinds of grimy grease and dust can build up here, eventually making it impossible for the refrigerator to keep cool enough. The cure is simply to clean the area. A fourth possibility is that the switch in the door has broken. This is usually operated by a button that is depressed when the door closes. Press it with your fingers and see if the light goes out—if it doesn't, call the repairman.

Refrigerator is very noisy: This is generally the result of the refrigerator not being perfectly level or of being wobbly. Screw the corner bases on which the refrigerator sits ④ in or out until everything is level and stable again.

Refrigerator is excessively frosted, or wet inside: These apparently opposite effects are often the result of the same problem—ice forming around the evaporator pan or clogging up the small drain holes. All that needs to be done is a defrosting.

Unstable interior temperatures: It is possible that the thermostat needs to be replaced, but more often the reason you have to continually adjust it is that the door is left open too long, the weather is unusually hot, or there simply isn't enough space around the refrigerator to allow proper air circulation. Try moving the refrigerator out a little.

A tip on moving the refrigerator: drop a rope made into a lasso around the refrigerator and lower it almost all the way to the bottom, and then pull. This way the refrigerator will slide, and not tip! Similarly, push it from the bottom rather than from the top.

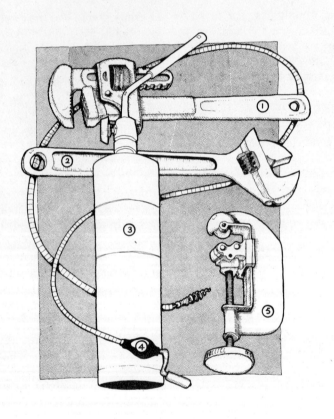

PROFESSIONAL HELP

Knowing how to do a particular job does not necessarily preclude the possibility that you would rather call in a professional. This book has been written to give *you* the ability to assess the situation on discovering a particular emergency. After having dealt with the immediate crisis you may decide that you would rather not risk going onto the roof yourself without the equipment that a professional roofer might use, or that the result of the repair is going to be very obvious and that only the skilled and practiced hands of a professional carpenter can do the job both effectively *and* without damaging the existing decor.

Against these and similar arguments you must weigh factors such as how long you will have to wait for a plumber's appointment, and how much more cheaply you might be able to do the job yourself. Of course, even the handiest person will still call in outside help from time to time, even if only because he is temporarily indisposed, or because some other business is making more pressing demands on his time.

Therefore, space is provided here for you to make and keep a list of emergency phone numbers. This way, when an emergency occurs, you can reach for this book, assess the situation, and, if the need exists, be able to locate the plumber, the electrician, the carpenter, the various servicemen for a house's different appliances and systems, and even the police and the fire department.

It might also be a good place to list your insurance company—and keep a record of repairs done and emergencies that have arisen and been dealt with (hopefully successfully) in the past. The old Latin proverb *experientia docet* is very true, but you must be able to remember and call upon the experience to be able to benefit from it.

INDEX

INDEX

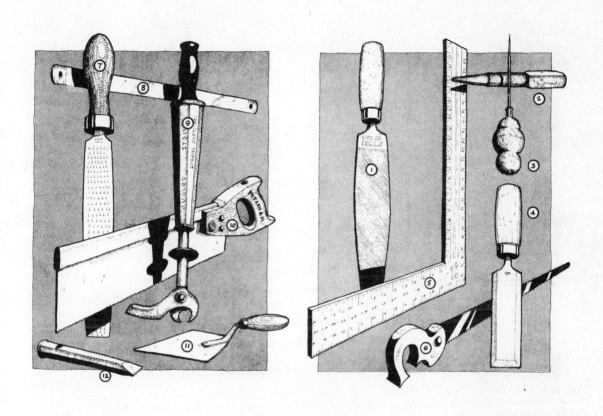